Eyewitness
FLYING MACHINE

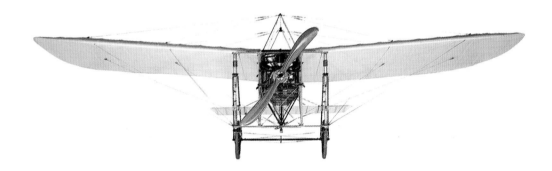

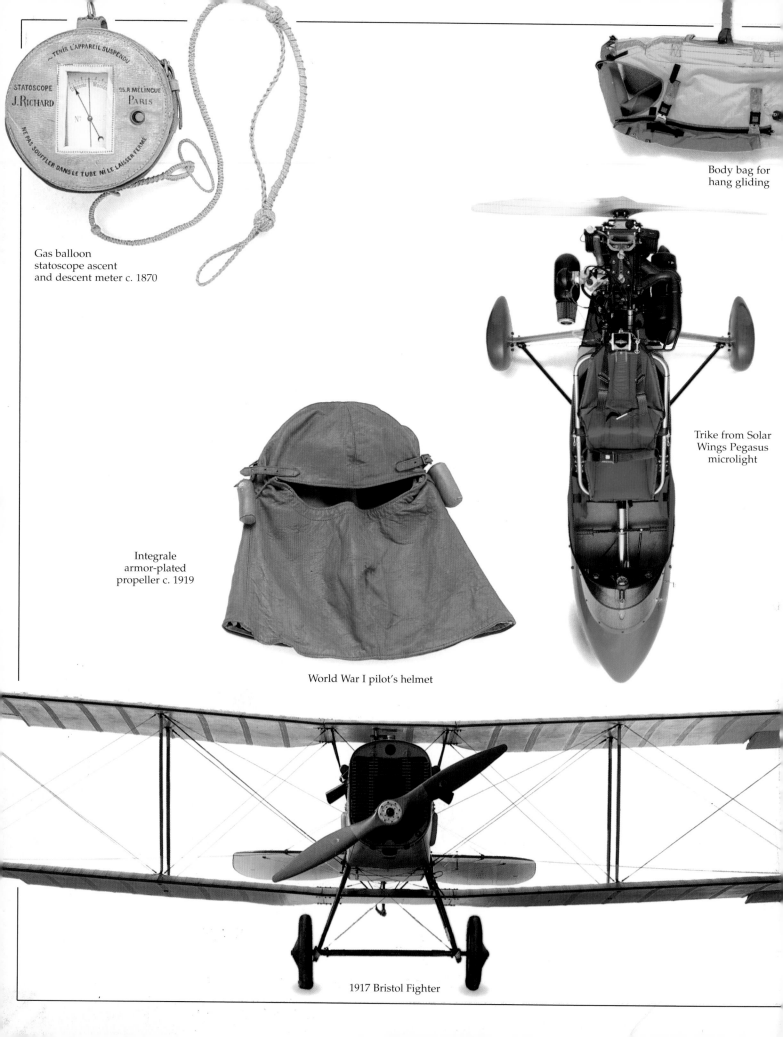

Gas balloon
statoscope ascent
and descent meter c. 1870

Body bag for
hang gliding

Trike from Solar
Wings Pegasus
microlight

Integrale
armor-plated
propeller c. 1919

World War I pilot's helmet

1917 Bristol Fighter

Spring pressure
airspeed indicator
c. 1910

Eyewitness
FLYING
MACHINE

Written by
ANDREW NAHUM

1982 Schleicher K23
single-seat glider

"Black box"
flight data recorder

Elliott pocket
altimeter c. 1910

1910 Anzani
"fan" engine

1927 Hawker Hart
pressed-steel
landing wheel

DK

DK Publishing, Inc.

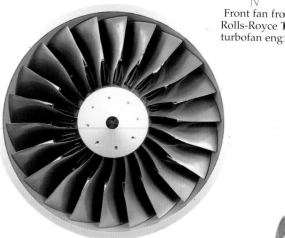

Front fan from
Rolls-Royce T
turbofan eng

LONDON, NEW YORK, MELBOURNE,
MUNICH, and DELHI

Undercarriage
from 1909
Deperdussin

Project editor John Farndon
Art editor Mark Richards
Managing editor Sophie Mitchell
Senior art editor Julia Harris
Editorial director Sue Unstead
Art director Anne-Marie Bulat
Special photography Dave King,
Peter Chadwick, and Mike Dunning

1909 Paragon
experimental
propeller blade

Mach meter c. 1960

REVISED EDITION
Managing editor Andrew Macintyre
Managing art editor Jane Thomas
Category publisher Linda Martin
Art director Simon Webb
Editor and reference compiler Sue Nicholson
Art editor Andrew Nash
Production Jenny Jacoby
Picture research Carolyn Clerkin
DTP designer Siu Yin Ho

U.S. editor Elizabeth Hester
Senior editor Beth Sutinis
Art director Dirk Kaufman
U.S. DTP designer Milos Orlovic
U.S. production Chris Avgherinos

This Eyewitness ® Guide has been conceived by
Dorling Kindersley Limited and Editions Gallimard

This edition published in the United States in 2004
by DK Publishing, Inc., 375 Hudson Street, New York, NY 10014

06 07 08 10 9 8 7 6 5 4 3

A catalog record for this book is
available from the Library of Congress.

ISBN 10: 0-7566-0680-2 ISBN 13: 978-0-7566-0680-0 (PLC)
ISBN 10: 0-7566-0679-9 ISBN 13: 978-0-7566-0679-4 (ALB)

Color reproduction by Colourscan, Singapore
Printed in China by Toppan Printing Co.,
(Shenzhen) Ltd.

Cockpit
from 1909
Deperdussin

Engine
parts from
Henson and
Stringfellow's
Aerial Steam
Carriage
of 1845

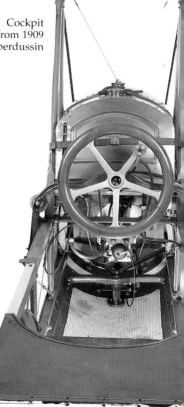

Discover more at
www.dk.com

Contents

World War I
goggles

Flying like a bird

SINCE THE DAYS of the mythical birdman Daedalus in ancient Greece, people have longed to fly like birds. For centuries, some believed that if they could mimic birds and their flapping wings, they too would be able to fly. During the Middle Ages in Europe, many a reckless experimenter strapped on wings and lunged into the air from towers and cliff tops – only to plummet to the ground, often fatally. Then, in the 15th century, the brilliant Italian artist and thinker Leonardo da Vinci applied his mind to unlocking the secrets of flight. Leonardo also believed that people could learn how to fly from birds. But he realized that human arms are too weak to flap wings for long, so he sketched designs for flapping wing machines, or "ornithopters." Centuries later, these sketches were discovered in his notebooks. As far as we know, Leonardo never tried to build his machines and, sadly, they would never have flown; imitating bird flight is far more complicated than even Leonardo understood. But his ideas represent one of the earliest scientific attempts to invent a flying machine.

FLYING DUCKS
In 1678, a French locksmith named Besnier tried to fly with wings that worked like the webbed feet of a duck. He was lucky to land alive.

THE FIRST FLYING ACCIDENT?
In ancient Greek legend, Daedalus was the craftsman who built the fabulous labyrinth for King Minos of Crete. Once the labyrinth was built, Minos threw him into prison to keep him from revealing its secret. Daedalus escaped with his son, Icarus, by soaring into the air on feather and wax wings he had made. In his excitement, Icarus flew so high that the sun melted the wax and he plunged into the sea.

Sketches from Leonardo's notebooks

HOW A BIRD FLIES
Most would-be aviators – including Leonardo – assumed that birds propel themselves through the air by flapping their wings down and backward, like rowing a boat. In fact, bird flight is much more complicated.

IN THE IMAGE OF A BIRD
Leonardo's notebooks show how intently he studied birds to solve the riddle of flight – and how ingenious he was at devising mechanisms to flap the wings of his machines like a bird's. He thought birds used the tips of their wings to "squeeze" the air and propel themselves. So he sketched intricate hinges and pulleys for clenching the wingtips. But he was wrong about wingtips, and he never really understood how a bird's wings lift and propel it through the air.

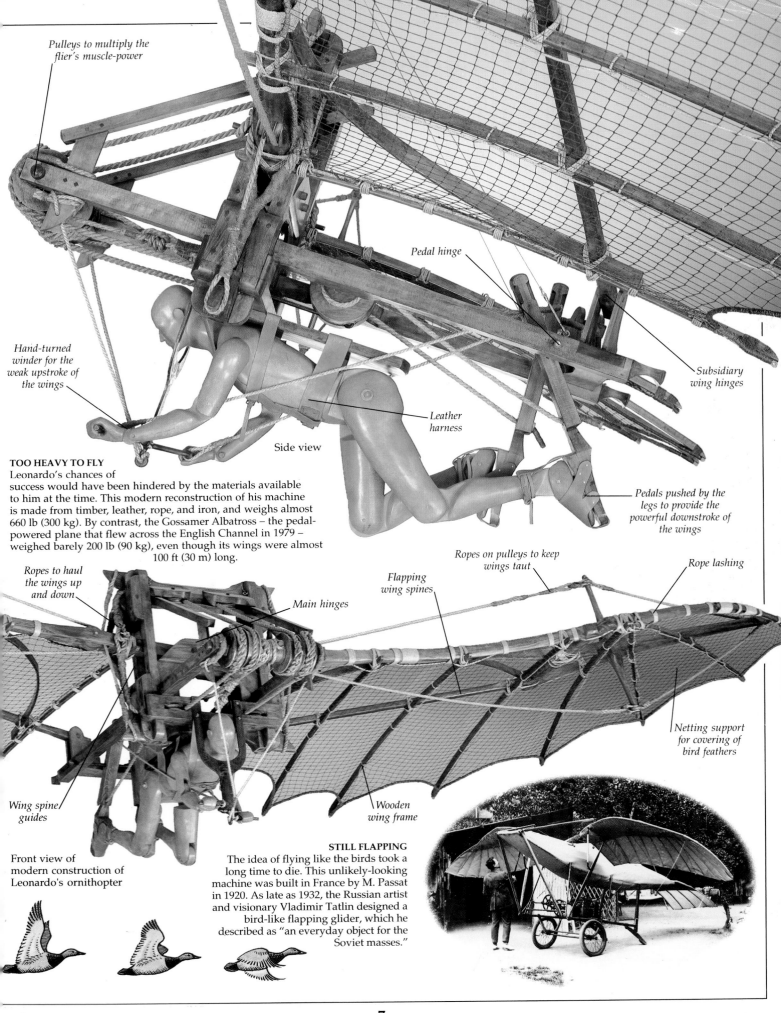

Pulleys to multiply the flier's muscle-power

Pedal hinge

Hand-turned winder for the weak upstroke of the wings

Subsidiary wing hinges

Leather harness

Side view

TOO HEAVY TO FLY
Leonardo's chances of
success would have been hindered by the materials available
to him at the time. This modern reconstruction of his machine
is made from timber, leather, rope, and iron, and weighs almost
660 lb (300 kg). By contrast, the Gossamer Albatross – the pedal-
powered plane that flew across the English Channel in 1979 –
weighed barely 200 lb (90 kg), even though its wings were almost
100 ft (30 m) long.

Pedals pushed by the legs to provide the powerful downstroke of the wings

Ropes on pulleys to keep wings taut

Rope lashing

Ropes to haul the wings up and down

Flapping wing spines

Main hinges

Netting support for covering of bird feathers

Wing spine guides

Wooden wing frame

Front view of modern construction of Leonardo's ornithopter

STILL FLAPPING
The idea of flying like the birds took a
long time to die. This unlikely-looking
machine was built in France by M. Passat
in 1920. As late as 1932, the Russian artist
and visionary Vladimir Tatlin designed a
bird-like flapping glider, which he
described as "an everyday object for the
Soviet masses."

Lighter than air

Hoop or load ring suspended from a net looped over the gas envelope

IT WAS NOT WINGS like a bird's that carried man aloft for the first time but a bubble of air. People had long believed that a balloon filled with a gas that was lighter than air would float. The problem was to find this gas. In fact, the first solution was simply hot air – because hot air is less dense (and so lighter) than cool air. In 1783, the French Montgolfier brothers made a huge paper balloon and filled it with hot air. In front of astonished Parisians, it rose majestically into the air, carrying two men. Within two weeks, a second historic balloon flight was made over Paris, this time by Jacques Charles and Maurice Robert. Their rubberized silk balloon was filledwith hydrogen gas instead of hot air, and this was to prove much more practical.

THE FIRST FLIGHT
On November 21, 1783, Francois de Rozier and the Marquis d'Arlandes became the world's first aeronauts, as the Montgolfier brothers' blue and gold balloon carried them into the air above Paris.

Short ropes suspending the basket from the load ring

FANTASTIC!
Over 400,000 people witnessed Charles's and Robert's historic flight, commemorated on this fan.

BALLOON MANIA
Parisian society went "balloon mad" and snapped up mementoes of the new wonder of the age, like this magic-lantern slide. Pulling the inner portion gave the illusion that the balloon was rising.

Strong rail to carry bags of sand ballast that were jettisoned (thrown overboard)to reduce weight and maintain height

SOCIAL CLIMBING
In the late 19th century, ballooning became a fashionable society sport, and well-to-do gentlemen would compete for distance and height records.

SOFT LANDING
Early balloons often hit the ground with a sickening thud. Some carried wicker cushions strapped below the balloon basket to soften the blow.

GAS BALLOON
Gas ballooning was popular throughout the 19th century because flights could last for hours – unlike hot-air flights, which were over as soon as the air cooled. Gas balloonists had two control lines – one to let out gas through a valve at the top of the balloon, for descending, and another to open the "ripping seam" to deflate the balloon once safely back on the ground.

Airships

The problem with balloons was that they simply floated where the wind took them. So in 1852, Henri Giffard made a cigar-shaped balloon and powered it with a steam engine to make it "dirigible" or steerable. Later, with gasoline engines and rigid-framed envelopes, these "airships" were the first large aircraft. By the 1920s, vast airships were carrying people across the Atlantic in ocean liner style. But a series of disasters caused by the flammable hydrogen gas spelled the end for airships.

SHIPS IN THE NIGHT
The sight of vast airships looming right over the heart of the city could be awe inspiring.

ZEPPELIN *below*
The German Zeppelin company led the world in airship-building. But its giant airship *Hindenburg*, 800 ft (245 m) long, was destroyed in a terrible accident on May 6, 1937, killing 35 passengers.

RIDING HIGH
Balloon races were very popular in the late 1800s. Professional aeronauts would often ride the load ring to make more room in the basket for joy-riding clients.

The *Hindenburg* and a modern jumbo jet to the same scale

Pocket barometer c .1909

UP AND DOWN *left*
To keep the balloon at a steady altitude, bags of sand ballast had to be jettisoned (thrown overboard) to make up for the gradual seeping of gas from the envelope. But the balance was delicate. Throwing out too much ballast made the balloon climb, forcing the aeronaut to let out more gas - not only to bring the balloon back down but also to vent gas, which expands at higher altitude. Constant venting of gas and jettisoning of ballast cut flights short, so early balloonists always carried sensitive barometric (pressure-controlled) statoscopes to tell them whether their balloons were rising or falling.

STATOSCOPE
J. Richard — 25.R.MÉLINGUE
PARIS
TENIR L'APPAREIL SUSPENDU
NE PAS SOUFFLER DANS LE TUBE NI LE LAISSER FERMÉ

Statoscope c .1870

Statoscope c .1900

Anchor to secure the balloon during inflation

MAKING GAS
The hydrogen gas to fill balloons was made by dripping sulfuric acid on iron shavings in contraptions like this.

Basket made of wicker for lightness and to absorb shocks

GAS DETECTOR
Hydrogen is so flammable that meters were used to detect leaks.

Gliding aloft

FOR A WHILE it seemed the future of flight lay with balloons and lighter-than-air craft. But British engineer Sir George Cayley thought otherwise. He was convinced that wings, too, would one day carry people into the air, drawing his inspiration from a familiar toy, the kite. Ingenious experiments with kites taught Cayley so much about how wings are lifted on the air that he was able to build a human-size version – the world's first real glider. Soon, other would-be aviators were trying their luck with gliders. It was all hit or miss, though, because no-one had any real idea how to control their craft in the air. Then, in the 1890s, a young German named Otto Lilienthal built a series of small, fragile gliders – much like modern hang gliders – and succeeded in making regular, controlled flights in them. His example proved crucial, and he has rightly been called the "world's first true aviator."

Tailplane

THE OLDEST AIRCRAFT?
Kites were probably flown in China over 3,000 years ago, but didn't reach Europe until the 14th century.

HANGING IN THE AIR
Photographs of Lilienthal gliding were published around the world, inspiring many imitators. His approach to flying was very scientific; he studied each problem with an analytical eye and tested each solution critically. Aviators should learn to glide, he insisted, to be "on intimate terms with the air" before taking the risky step of trying out a motor – advice that was crucial to the success of the Wright brothers (p. 14).

Sir George Cayley

The invention of the airplane owes a great deal to the pioneering work of the English engineer Sir George Cayley (1773-1857). It was Cayley who first worked out how a wing works, and all modern aircraft are based on the kitelike model glider he built in 1804, with its up-angled front wing and stabilizing tail. In 1853, at the age of 80, he built a full-size glider which is said to have carried his terrified coachman in a flight across a small valley.

Sir George Cayley

PLANE IDEAS *below*
Cayley had ideas for many different flying machines, including an airship and this passenger-carrying glider, which he called a "governable parachute".

Wing cover of unvarnished cotton

Replica of Lilienthal's No. 11 hang glider of 1895

Wing moving toward the right of the page, with airflow shown in blue and vertical arrow showing lift

HOW A WING WORKS

Wings are lifted by the air flowing above and below them as they cut through the air. Air pushed over the top speeds up and is stretched out, so that pressure above the wing lessens. But air flowing beneath slows and its pressure increases. So, in effect, the wing is sucked from above and pushed from below. Even a flat board can give some lift, but pioneers like Lilienthal discovered that a curved or "cambered" surface is best. Today, wings are thicker and far more effective than those of the pioneers. Research with computers and wind tunnels ensures the best shape for each type of aircraft.

TRAGIC ACCIDENT

Sadly, Lilienthal was killed in 1896 while flying one of his gliders. The accident occurred not in town as suggested by this engraving but in open country near Berlin, when a gust of wind threw the glider out of control.

BRACED PAIR

The Wright brothers (p. 14) adopted the same braced construction as this biplane (double wing) built by French-American Octave Chanute in the mid-1890s.

Wooden spars to keep wing shape

Willow hoop to act as shock absorber

Lilienthal supported himself on his forearms and controlled the glider by swinging his legs to shift its center of gravity

Willow ribs

BELL'S KITE

Many pioneers believed that big human-carrying kites had a future. This one was designed by Alexander Graham Bell, inventor of the telephone.

Powered flight

WITH A GLIDER, it was at last possible to fly on wings – but not for long. To fly any real distance, an engine was needed. By as early as 1845, two Englishmen, William Henson and John Stringfellow, had built a working model of a plane powered by a specially made lightweight steam engine – the only engine then available. Nobody knows whether their model ever really got off the ground, but it showed that the idea of a powered flying machine was no longer just a dream. Over the next 50 years, many imaginative engineers tried to get steam-powered flying machines airborne, both models and full-size airplanes. But steam engines proved either too weak or too heavy, and it wasn't until the invention of compact gas engines that powered flight became a real possibility.

EAGLE POWER
People had long known that a little more than human power was needed to fly. . .

"All-moving tailplane," or elevator

Silk-covered wings with 20 ft (6 m) span

Boiler

Wing brace

Engine pulley

Rudder

Connecting rod

Steam tube

Cylinder and piston

STEAM POWER
Henson and Stringfellow built a special lightweight steam engine for their model, with a boiler no longer than 10 in (25 cm). Heat for the engine came from a naphtha or alcohol burner, and steam was produced in the row of conical tubes. (In the full-size version, the boiler would have had 50 of these tubes, but the engine was never built.) Steam from the boiler drove the piston up and down, turning the wooden pulley. This, in turn, spun the two propellers via a twine drive belt.

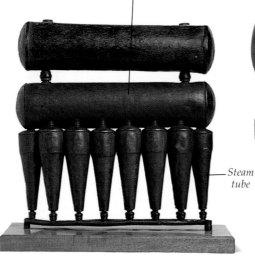

DID IT FLY?
Stringfellow built another model in 1848. To launch it, he ran it down a sloping wire for 33 ft (10 m) and then released it with the engine running. Some accounts say the model showed true powered flight by climbing a little before it hit a wall.

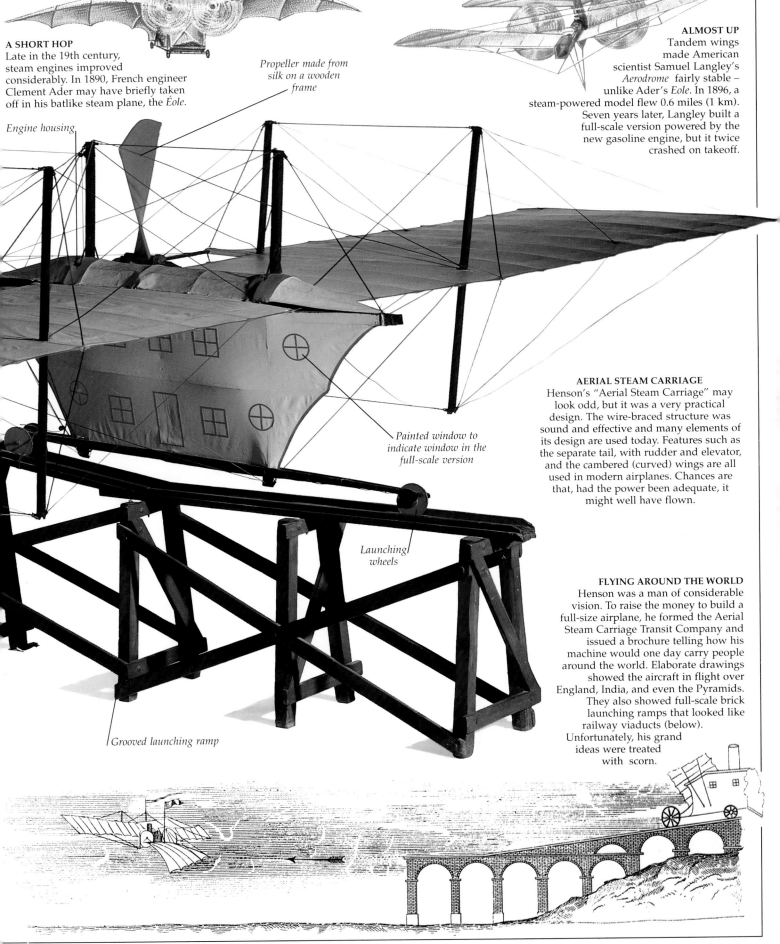

A SHORT HOP
Late in the 19th century, steam engines improved considerably. In 1890, French engineer Clement Ader may have briefly taken off in his batlike steam plane, the *Éole*.

Engine housing

Propeller made from silk on a wooden frame

ALMOST UP
Tandem wings made American scientist Samuel Langley's *Aerodrome* fairly stable – unlike Ader's *Éole*. In 1896, a steam-powered model flew 0.6 miles (1 km). Seven years later, Langley built a full-scale version powered by the new gasoline engine, but it twice crashed on takeoff.

Painted window to indicate window in the full-scale version

AERIAL STEAM CARRIAGE
Henson's "Aerial Steam Carriage" may look odd, but it was a very practical design. The wire-braced structure was sound and effective and many elements of its design are used today. Features such as the separate tail, with rudder and elevator, and the cambered (curved) wings are all used in modern airplanes. Chances are that, had the power been adequate, it might well have flown.

Launching wheels

FLYING AROUND THE WORLD
Henson was a man of considerable vision. To raise the money to build a full-size airplane, he formed the Aerial Steam Carriage Transit Company and issued a brochure telling how his machine would one day carry people around the world. Elaborate drawings showed the aircraft in flight over England, India, and even the Pyramids. They also showed full-scale brick launching ramps that looked like railway viaducts (below). Unfortunately, his grand ideas were treated with scorn.

Grooved launching ramp

The first airplanes

Wing made by stretching linen over a wooden frame and treating it to shrink it tight

ONE COLD THURSDAY in December 1903, at Kitty Hawk North Carolina, the gasoline-powered flying machine built by the brothers Orville and Wilbur Wright rose unsteadily into the air, flew 120 ft (40 m), then returned safely to the ground again. The world's first powered, sustained, and controlled aeroplane flight had been made. At first, reports of the Wrights' achievement were met with disbelief in Europe, but their success was no accident. They had been methodically improving their designs – and, crucially, their flying skill – since 1899. When Wilbur brought the *Flyer* to France in 1908, it was clear that the Wrights were far ahead of the pioneers in Europe. But aviation was now progressing everywhere rapidly. Sustained flights were soon almost routine. Then, in 1909, Frenchman Louis Blériot flew one of his little aircraft 26 miles (41 km) right over the English Channel from France to England.

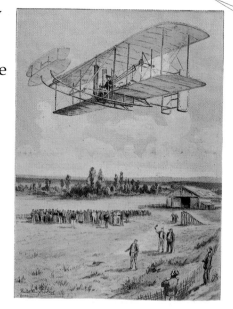

THE WRIGHTS' *FLYER* *above*
The Wrights realized that their plane needed some form of control to stop it rolling from side to side. So the *Flyer* had wires to "warp" (twist) the wings to lift one side or the other. This meant it could not only fly level but also make balanced, banked turns, rather like a bicycle cornering.

Pilot's cockpit

Landing gear with elastic shock-absorbing cord

Wing warp control wires

Side view of Blériot Type XI

BLÉRIOT TYPE XI
Louis Blériot's first attempts to fly, from 1905 on, were disaster filled, and he crashed several times. But he pioneered the soon familiar "monoplane" aircraft with a single wing, separate tail, and engine in front. Then, in 1908, inspired by the Wrights' control over their plane, he added wing warping to his planes with highly successful results. The Blériot Type XI shown above is identical to the plane in which he flew over the English Channel on July 25, 1909 (left).

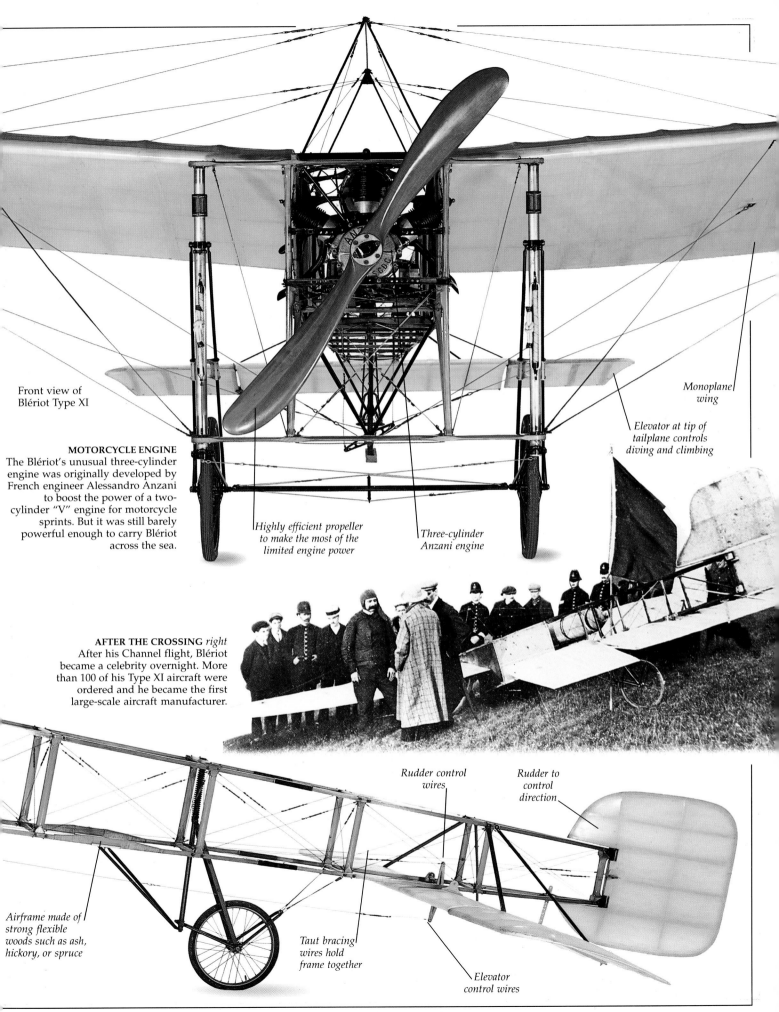

Front view of
Blériot Type XI

MOTORCYCLE ENGINE
The Blériot's unusual three-cylinder engine was originally developed by French engineer Alessandro Anzani to boost the power of a two-cylinder "V" engine for motorcycle sprints. But it was still barely powerful enough to carry Blériot across the sea.

Highly efficient propeller to make the most of the limited engine power

Three-cylinder Anzani engine

Monoplane wing

Elevator at tip of tailplane controls diving and climbing

AFTER THE CROSSING *right*
After his Channel flight, Blériot became a celebrity overnight. More than 100 of his Type XI aircraft were ordered and he became the first large-scale aircraft manufacturer.

Rudder control wires

Rudder to control direction

Airframe made of strong flexible woods such as ash, hickory, or spruce

Taut bracing wires hold frame together

Elevator control wires

15

Those magnificent men

THE FEATS OF THE WRIGHTS, Blériot, and various other brave and inventive pioneers created tremendous excitement, and aviation emerged as the sensation of the age. The daring young men who demonstrated their flying skill at air shows quickly became superstars. When a Parisian theater audience found in its midst Adolphe Pégoud – one of the first pilots to perform aerobatics and loops – they stopped the show until he gave them a talk on aviation! Another pioneer pilot, Louis Paulhan, was said to have earned a fortune from his flying exploits. The early fliers certainly earned their fame, for their planes were difficult and dangerous to fly and accidents were frequent. Sitting on an exposed seat was also uncomfortable and very, very cold. Warm clothing was absolutely vital. When Blériot crossed the Channel, he wore overalls, but special flying gear was soon developed.

Soft "chrome" leather

Warm wool lining

FINDING THE WAY
In the early days, pilots navigated by flying straight toward landmarks. A good set of maps was invaluable.

HOT FOOT
Warm boots were essential. These are soft sheepskin-lined boots, originally thigh-length but cut down by the owner for convenience.

Thick rubber sole gave good grip when climbing aboard the aircraft

"WINDPROOF AIRMAN KIT"
This suit from around 1911 could be lined with either fleece or quilt.

Flying gear c. 1916

World War I spurred the rapid development of flying gear. This selection was issued to pilots of the British Royal Flying Corps. Leather was thought the best material at the time, but was soon replaced by one-piece suits of waxed cotton lined with silk and fur (Sidcot suits).

Fold-up collar to keep neck warm

Goggle-holders

HEAD IN THE CLOUDS
Cowl-type helmets with face masks like this were sometimes used for high-altitude flying. But some "aces" felt more alert flying without either helmet or goggles.

GOGGLE-EYED
For most pilots, goggles gave vital eye protection against the wind. This pair is tinted to reduce glare and made with anti-splinter glass.

Leather gloves lined with sheepskin

HANDS IN THE AIR
Stuck out in the airstream on the controls, hands could quickly suffer frostbite if not protected by warm gloves.

Button-up cuffs to keep out wind

WINDPROOF
Higher speeds and longer flights in World War I meant suits had to be more windproof, particularly at the neck, wrists, and ankles.

Double wings

THE EARLIEST PLANES had one, two, three, and sometimes more sets of wings, and each arrangement had its supporters. But Blériot's cross-Channel flight in 1909 (pp. 14-15) showed just how effective a monoplane (single-winger) could be. Over the next few years, monoplanes tended to dominate in air races – since multiwinged planes were slowed more by air-resistance (drag).

Unfortunately, these overstressed, competition monoplanes were much too accident-prone and, in 1912, the French and British army authorities decided to ban monoplanes altogether. They feared the single wing was weak – since, to give a lifting area equal to multiwings, a single wing had to be very long. The best compromise between strength and low wind resistance seemed to be biplanes (two wingers). So when World War I began, almost all the fighters and observation planes were biplanes. The demands of war gave a tremendous boost to aircraft development. By the time the war was over, the airplane was a relatively sophisticated and reliable machine.

Radiator for engine-cooling water

Wooden propeller

Small propeller to drive the pump that supplies fuel to the engine

FOKKER TRIPLANE
Some triplanes (three wingers) were built during the war. The famous German wartime Fokker Triplane was said to climb like an elevator. It was also highly maneuverable. But drag (air resistance) slowed triplanes down, and by 1917 no air force was using them at all.

IMMELMANN TURN
The dogfights of World War I revealed just how maneuverable planes had become in a short time. The Immelmann turn was said to be a favourite way for pilots to evade pursuit or mount a hit-and-run attack. But it is unlikely that fighter pilot Max Immelmann or any other flying "ace" would have made himself so vulnerable by flying upside down in front of the enemy's guns. It was probably just a simple steep climbing turn.

8-cylinder 300 hp
Hispano-Suiza V
engine

Vickers forward-firing
machine gun aimed through
a hole in the radiator

Timing device to
ensure that gun fires
through the propeller
only when the blades
are horizontal

Control stick for
climbing, diving,
and banking

Pilot's seat

Rudder
control
wires

Rudder bar

Fuel tank

Ash
frame

Bracing struts

Light wire
landing wheels

Wing stubs

FIGHTING LIKE DOGS
"Dogfights" were fought
between single-seat patrol
planes with forward-firing
machine guns. Since the pilot
had to aim the whole aircraft
at the enemy to shoot, flying
skill was vital.

Bristol Fighter
c. 1917

In the early years of the war, the
dangerous work of artillery
spotting and observation
was performed by
slow two seaters,
often protected
by faster single
seaters. When
the British Bristol
Fighter came on
the scene in 1917,
however, its powerful
engine made it fast enough
to act as both spotter and fighter.

Continued on next page

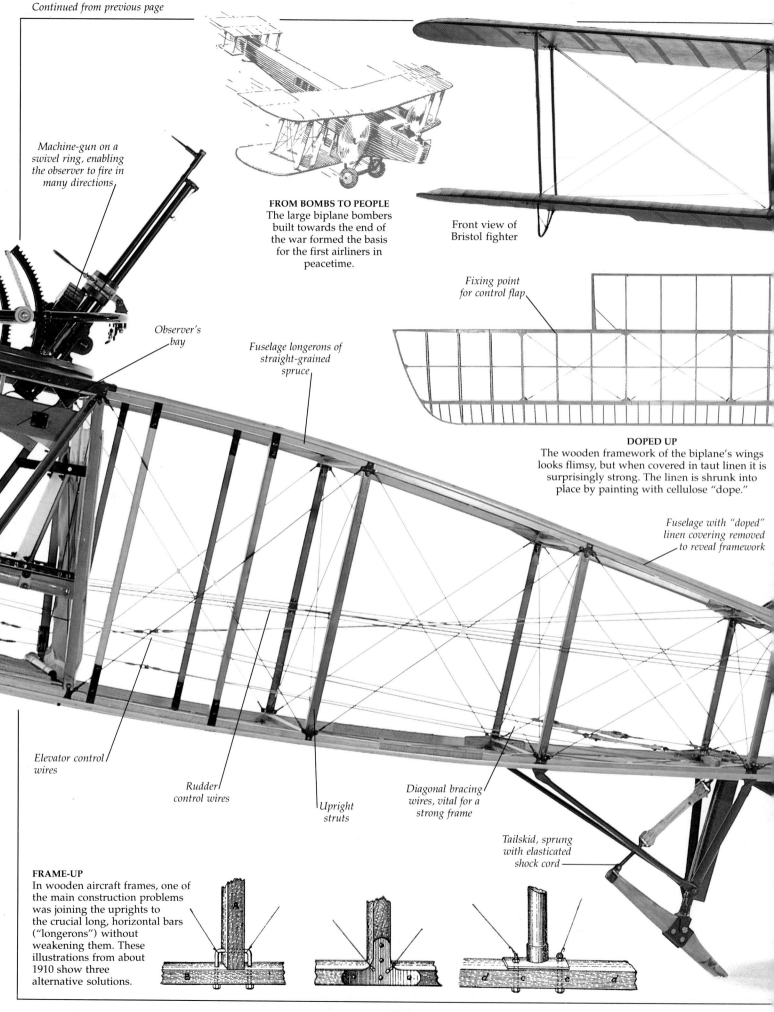

Machine-gun on a swivel ring, enabling the observer to fire in many directions

FROM BOMBS TO PEOPLE
The large biplane bombers built towards the end of the war formed the basis for the first airliners in peacetime.

Front view of Bristol fighter

Fixing point for control flap

DOPED UP
The wooden framework of the biplane's wings looks flimsy, but when covered in taut linen it is surprisingly strong. The linen is shrunk into place by painting with cellulose "dope."

Observer's bay

Fuselage longerons of straight-grained spruce

Fuselage with "doped" linen covering removed to reveal framework

Elevator control wires

Rudder control wires

Upright struts

Diagonal bracing wires, vital for a strong frame

Tailskid, sprung with elasticated shock cord

FRAME-UP
In wooden aircraft frames, one of the main construction problems was joining the uprights to the crucial long, horizontal bars ("longerons") without weakening them. These illustrations from about 1910 show three alternative solutions.

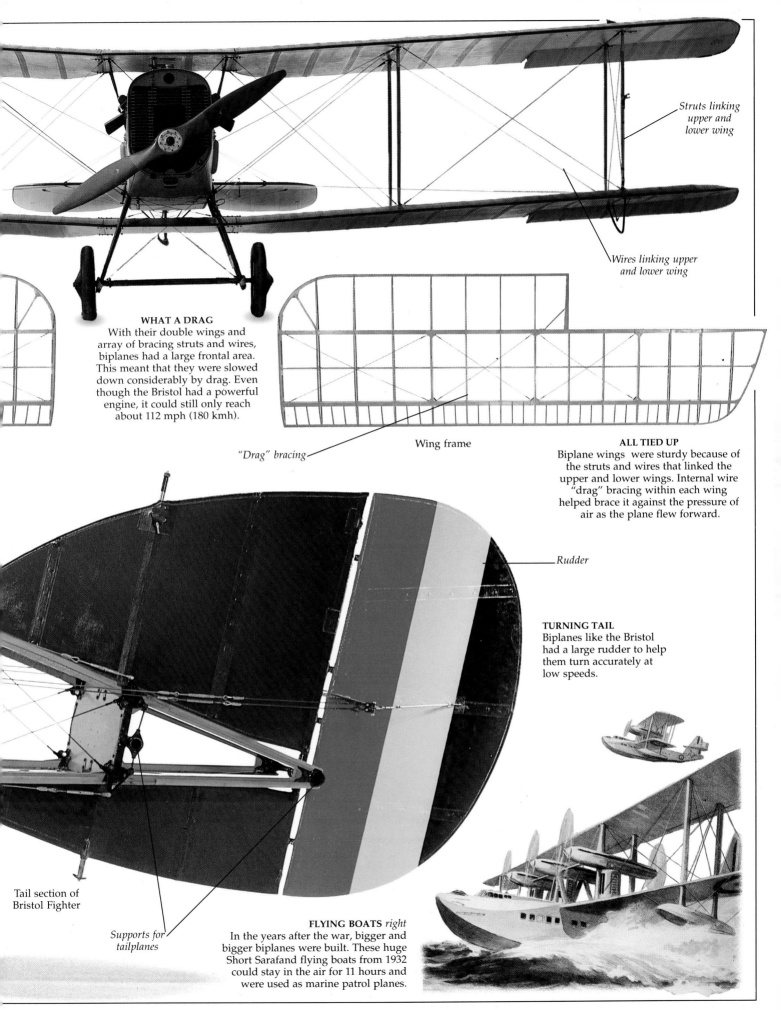

**Struts linking
upper and
lower wing**

**Wires linking upper
and lower wing**

WHAT A DRAG
With their double wings and
array of bracing struts and wires,
biplanes had a large frontal area.
This meant that they were slowed
down considerably by drag. Even
though the Bristol had a powerful
engine, it could still only reach
about 112 mph (180 kmh).

"Drag" bracing

Wing frame

ALL TIED UP
Biplane wings were sturdy because of
the struts and wires that linked the
upper and lower wings. Internal wire
"drag" bracing within each wing
helped brace it against the pressure of
air as the plane flew forward.

Rudder

TURNING TAIL
Biplanes like the Bristol
had a large rudder to help
them turn accurately at
low speeds.

Tail section of
Bristol Fighter

*Supports for
tailplanes*

FLYING BOATS *right*
In the years after the war, bigger and
bigger biplanes were built. These huge
Short Sarafand flying boats from 1932
could stay in the air for 11 hours and
were used as marine patrol planes.

The evolving plane

IN THE 20 YEARS after the first international airshow was held at Reims in France in August 1909, aviation progressed at an astonishing rate. The airplanes of 1909 were mostly slow, frail machines with flimsy, open, wood frames, low-powered engines and rudimentary controls. No plane at the airshow flew faster than 47 mph (75 kmh) nor climbed higher than 500 ft (150 m) or so above the ground. Yet, within four years, aircraft were flying over 120 mph (200 kmh), climbing to 20,000 ft (6000 m) and performing aerobatic feats such as loops and rolls (p. 41). By 1929, ungainly wooden planes were almost a thing of the past, and new all-metal planes with streamlined fuselages and wings were tearing across the sky at previously undreamed-of speeds.

DEPERDUSSIN 1909
Deperdussin was among the most advanced aircraft manufacturers in the years before World War I, and its sleek monoplanes took many speed records. Nevertheless, this example shows many features typical of the pioneering planes, with lateral control by wing warping (p. 14), a low-powered engine, and extensive wire bracing.

King-post acts as anchor point for the rigging wires to the wings

Brass tank positioned high to feed fuel to the engine simply through gravity

Rigging wires to hold the monoplane wing

35 hp Anzani radial engine ran smoother than the fan engine fitted to the Blériot (p. 15)

Flexible monoplane wings

Wing-warp control cable

Rocking crank

Rigging wires become taut in flight as the wing lifts

Wires from rocking crank to warp the wings

Landing gear struts forming important part of aircraft structure

SOPWITH PUP 1917

Aircraft improved immeasurably in the years before World War I, and wartime biplane fighters were faster and much more maneuverable than the flying machines of the pioneers. Lightweight rotary engines (pp. 28-29) propelled fighters like this Sopwith Pup along at speeds of 115 mph (185 kmh) or more, and improved control allowed them to engage in dramatic aerial dogfights. To bank the plane, the pilot no longer warped the wings but raised or lowered hinged flaps called "ailerons" on the tips of strong, rigid wings (pp. 40-41). Fuselages, by now, were always enclosed and, towards the end of the war, a few aircraft manufacturers began to experiment with "monocoques" in which all the strength came from a single shell rather than internal struts and bracing.

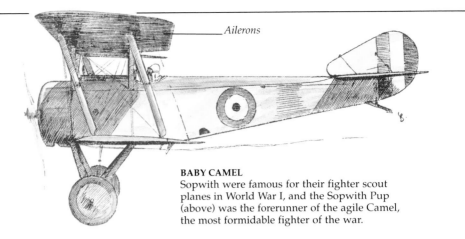

Ailerons

BABY CAMEL
Sopwith were famous for their fighter scout planes in World War I, and the Sopwith Pup (above) was the forerunner of the agile Camel, the most formidable fighter of the war.

Gunsight

Vickers machine gun

Aluminum engine cowling to catch all the oil thrown out by a rotary engine

Streamlined struts

100 hp Gnome rotary engine

Sophisticated arrangement of bracing wires gives very strong structure essential for dogfights

Exhaust slot

Efficient cambered wing

Continued on next page

Continued from previous page

HAWKER HART 1927

Near the end of World War I, wood shortages persuaded many plane makers to experiment with metal, and they soon realized that metal was actually superior in many ways. Throughout the 1920s, air forces still preferred biplanes to monoplanes for their robustness, good handling, and low landing speeds. But fabric and wood wings were now frequently combined with metal monocoque fuselages. By the end of the decade, very powerful engines and a more streamlined shape for both wings and fuselage meant that even biplanes could hurtle through the air at over 200 mph (320 kmh).

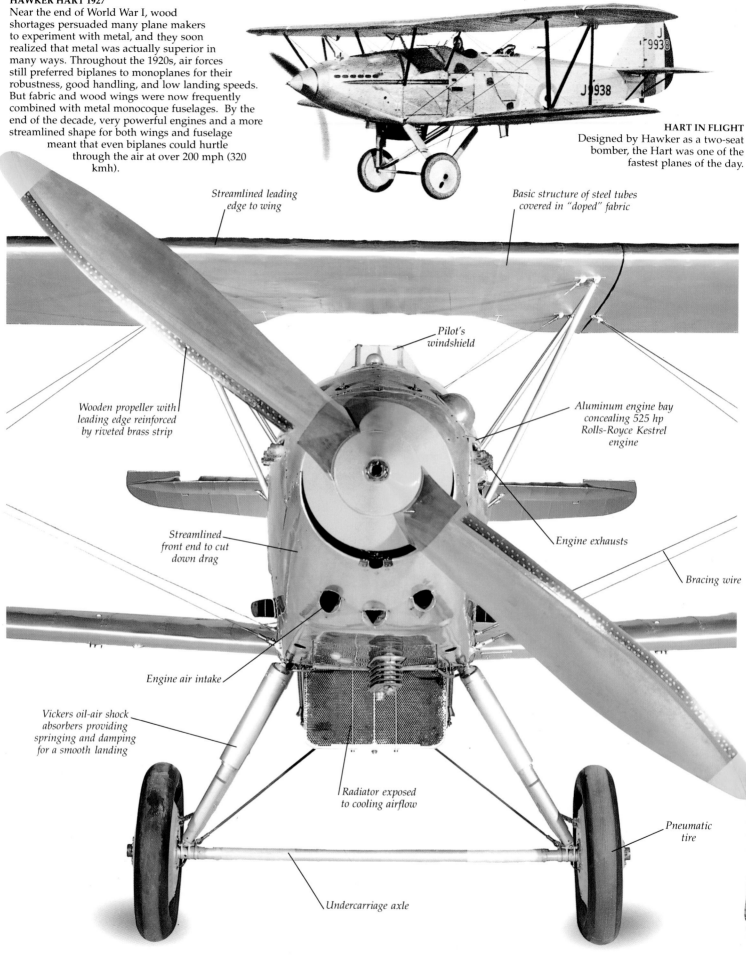

HART IN FLIGHT
Designed by Hawker as a two-seat bomber, the Hart was one of the fastest planes of the day.

Streamlined leading edge to wing

Basic structure of steel tubes covered in "doped" fabric

Pilot's windshield

Aluminum engine bay concealing 525 hp Rolls-Royce Kestrel engine

Wooden propeller with leading edge reinforced by riveted brass strip

Streamlined front end to cut down drag

Engine exhausts

Bracing wire

Engine air intake

Vickers oil-air shock absorbers providing springing and damping for a smooth landing

Radiator exposed to cooling airflow

Pneumatic tire

Undercarriage axle

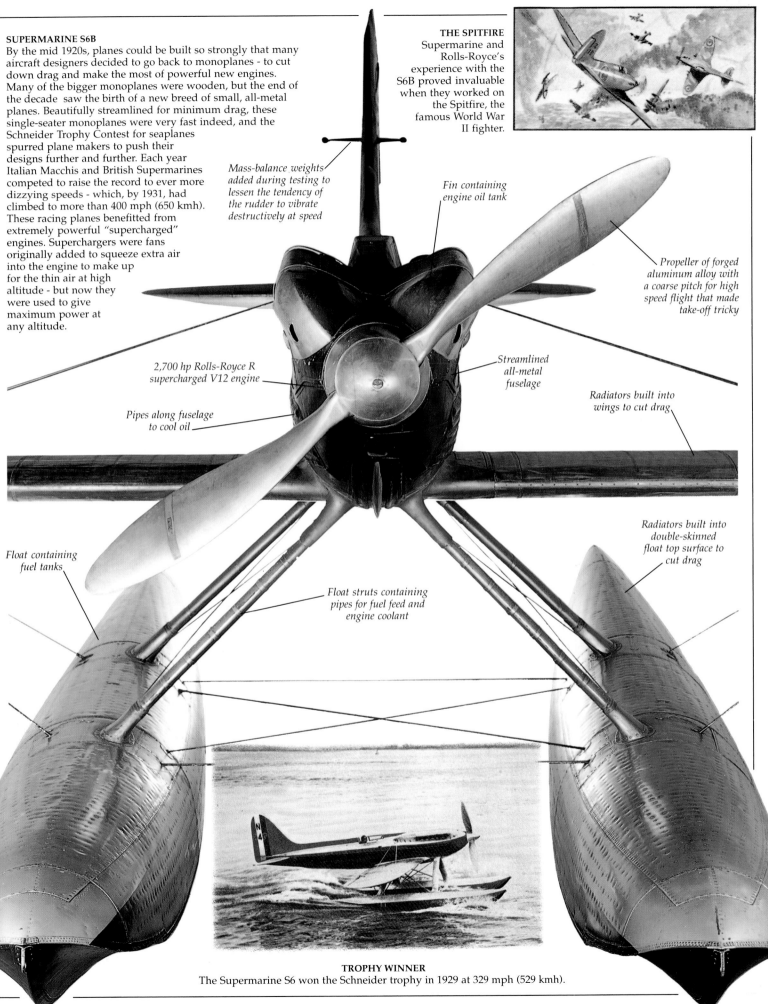

SUPERMARINE S6B

By the mid 1920s, planes could be built so strongly that many aircraft designers decided to go back to monoplanes - to cut down drag and make the most of powerful new engines. Many of the bigger monoplanes were wooden, but the end of the decade saw the birth of a new breed of small, all-metal planes. Beautifully streamlined for minimum drag, these single-seater monoplanes were very fast indeed, and the Schneider Trophy Contest for seaplanes spurred plane makers to push their designs further and further. Each year Italian Macchis and British Supermarines competed to raise the record to ever more dizzying speeds - which, by 1931, had climbed to more than 400 mph (650 kmh). These racing planes benefitted from extremely powerful "supercharged" engines. Superchargers were fans originally added to squeeze extra air into the engine to make up for the thin air at high altitude - but now they were used to give maximum power at any altitude.

THE SPITFIRE
Supermarine and Rolls-Royce's experience with the S6B proved invaluable when they worked on the Spitfire, the famous World War II fighter.

Mass-balance weights added during testing to lessen the tendency of the rudder to vibrate destructively at speed

Fin containing engine oil tank

Propeller of forged aluminum alloy with a coarse pitch for high speed flight that made take-off tricky

2,700 hp Rolls-Royce R supercharged V12 engine

Streamlined all-metal fuselage

Radiators built into wings to cut drag

Pipes along fuselage to cool oil

Radiators built into double-skinned float top surface to cut drag

Float containing fuel tanks

Float struts containing pipes for fuel feed and engine coolant

TROPHY WINNER
The Supermarine S6 won the Schneider trophy in 1929 at 329 mph (529 kmh).

Light aircraft

EPIC FLIGHT
The most famous light plane was the *Spirit of St. Louis* in which Charles Lindbergh flew solo across the Atlantic in 1927.

Today, light, single-engined light planes are used all over the world for training pilots, for transportation in and out of remote places and for recreational flying. They are very simple aircraft, usually, with fixed landing gear, a monoplane wing above the cabin, simple fuselage and tail, and a small gasoline engine to turn the propeller at the front. Typically conventional in design, they work in much the same way as the planes of the pioneers. Only the materials are genuinely new, with aluminum alloys and plastics replacing the traditional wood and linen.

Fuel tank holding enough fuel for 2.5 hours or 120 miles (190 km) flying

Tiny, two-cylinder, Rotax engine

SNOWBIRD
The basic shape of light planes has changed little since World War II, and the main elements of planes like the Snowbird have long been familiar to pilots. However, the Snowbird makes the most of modern developments in "microlights" (pp. 62-63). The result is a plane that is not only very light but costs little more than a family car.

GASOLINE POWER
While bigger, faster planes now usually have jet engines, gasoline engines are quite adequate for light planes.

Cabin superstructure of light aluminum, with roof forming wing mounts

Fixed landing gear

ON THE PANEL
On the Snowbird's instrument panel, digital electronic displays replace the clocks and cables traditionally used on light planes.

Wing front of alloy sheet in "D box" shape to resist twisting

WEIGHT LIFTER
Wings are specially designed for each plane to give just the right amount of lift; the length of the wing (its span) and its cross section (camber) are critical. Wings must be light and very strong too. The stresses placed on the wings of even the lightest, slowest plane as it flies through the air are considerable. The Snowbird's wing of fabric stretched over an aluminum frame is unusually simple, but the cross-struts and bracing pieces had to be very carefully designed.

Absence of ailerons makes wing frame very simple

AIRSCREW
Most light planes have a traditional twin-bladed propeller of laminated wood, mounted at the front to pull the plane forward.

PLANE AND SIMPLE
The high wing Cessna 172E Skyhawk is the classic all-purpose light plane used for training, leisure, and business. The body is all metal and a 160 hp flat four-cylinder engine propels it along at 137 mph (220 kmh).

LITTLE RACER
The basic layout for light planes – with high wings, engine in the nose and fixed wheels – was established back in the 1930s, when this Comper Swift was built. The Swift was one of the many light planes used for sport, and its Pobjoy seven-cylinder radial engine made it surprisingly fast. In 1933, it flew from Britain to Australia in record time.

Aluminum airframe

Fuselage

LONG BODY
In light planes, the main body – called the fuselage – is simply a tapered tube that supports the tailplane in exactly the right place in relation to the main wings. On some light planes, the fuselage is a strong, streamlined tube of welded steel. The slow-flying Snowbird needs only fabric stretched over a light, square aluminum frame.

BALANCE WING
The Wrights' *Flyer* had small wings on the front to help keep the plane flying level - yet on virtually every plane since, the stabilizing wings have been at the back and are called the tailplane. Without a tailplane, the aircraft would tilt up and down uncontrollably. On the tailplane's trailing (rear) edges are hinged flaps called elevators, which the pilot moves up or down to climb or dive (pp. 40-41).

Fin and rudder upright

Elevators

Tailplane

Aluminum rudder frame

Simple mid wing spoilers – not the usual ailerons – to control aircraft banking

Special plastic film , shrunk tight over the aircraft frame with a heat gun

TURNING TAIL
Every plane has an upright fin at the rear to keep it flying in a straight line. But the back end of the fin, called the rudder, swings like the rudder of a boat, to turn the plane left or right. Steering a plane in the air, however, is not as simple as steering a boat, and the pilot has to use the ailerons or spoilers on the main wings as well (pp. 40-41).

COMPLETE PLANE
The finished Snowbird is so light and stable that it stalls (stops flying) only when the speed drops as low as 34 mph (55 kmh) – half as fast as many small planes.

Airplane engines

VITAL SPARK
Like a car engine, aircraft piston engines have spark plugs to ignite the fuel charge to drive the piston down in each cylinder.

POWERED FLIGHT became a real possibility only with the development of piston engines for cars in the early years of the 20th century. Indeed, many pioneering machines were propelled into the air by engines taken straight from cars and motorcycles and modified by ingenious aviators. Unfortunately, air-cooled motorcycle engines often lost power or jammed in mid flight, and water-cooled car engines were very heavy. So before long, aviators began to build their own engines, engines both light and extremely powerful. From then on, piston engines for aircraft became more and more powerful and sophisticated. Soon after World War II, however, with the arrival of jet engines, piston engines were only needed in light planes.

Carburetor

Exhaust

Copper cooling jacket around the cylinder

Cylinder cut away to reveal piston

Pipe to carry a mixture of fuel and air from the carburetor to the cylinders

COOL JACKET
To save weight, some big water-cooled airplane engines, like this ENV from c. 1910, had very thin copper water jackets, coated electrically onto the cylinders.

Piston – driven down the cylinder by burning fuel and back up again by the rotating crankshaft

Crankcase containing crankshaft turned by the pistons

Flange for exhaust pipe

Cast-iron cylinders with fins to improve cooling by increasing the area of metal exposed to the airflow

WHEELS TO WINGS
Like many early airplane-engines, this 1910 Anzani "fan" type engine came from a motorcycle. Anzani had originally put the extra cylinder in the middle of its V-twin engine to gain power for motorcycle sprints and hill-climbs. This was the kind of engine used by Blériot for his Channel crossing in 1909. Its output of 25 hp was barely adequate for the task, and the engine would have jammed, so it is said, if a timely shower of rain had not cooled it down.

Float to control the level of fuel in the carburetor

Carburetor to deliver fuel to the cylinders at the right rate

Propeller mounted here and turned by the crankshaft

ROTARY ENGINE
The earliest airplane engines had cylinders in a row, and needed heavy water-cooling systems, or in a circle (radially), and did not cool well at all. So in 1909, the French Seguin brothers brought in the "rotary" engine. Like the radial engine, it had the cylinders in a ring. But unlike the radial, the cylinders went around with the propeller while the central crank stayed still.

Crankshaft stays still while the cylinders rotate around it

Inlet pipes channeling the fuel and air mixture from the crankcase to the cylinders

Valves to let fuel in and burned gases (exhaust) out

Cylinders kept especially cool by the flow of air around them as they rotate

Crankcase rotates with the cylinders

Finely machined cylinders with light, thin walls only 1 mm thick

Connecting rods to pistons all joined to a single bearing around the crankshaft

AIR-GIANT
Not all propeller planes were powered by piston engines. The huge Saunders-Roe Princess flying boat had six big "turboprop" jet engines (p. 36) to turn twelve propellers.

LIGHT POWER
Piston engines for light planes are now very light and compact. This Weslake weighs only 19 lb (8.4 kg) – yet pushes out as much power as Blériot's 1908 Anzani which weighed over 150 lb (70 kg).

Carburetor

Propeller shaft

Cylinder

The propeller

PROPELLERS seem to have changed little since the pioneering days. Yet as the Wright brothers were quick to appreciate, they are not simply oars for the air; they are like spinning wings that thrust the plane forward in much the same way as wings lift it upward. So the shape of a propeller is as crucial to performance as the shape of a wing, and the subtle evolution of propeller design over the years has improved efficiency dramatically. They have gained in strength, too, as construction has changed from laminations (layers) of wood to forged aluminum, to cope with steadily increasing engine power.

WRIGHT 1909
The Wright brothers built their own wind tunnel for testing wings and propellers. This design shows that they knew the blade had to be twisted to give it a shallower angle at the tip.

PHILLIPS 1893
This early propeller, designed by "airfoil" (wing shape) expert Horatio Phillips, looks like a ship's propeller. Yet it worked well, once lifting a tethered experimental aircraft weighing 400 lb (180 kg).

Propeller blade made from strips of wood

Blade angle (pitch) steeper closer to the hub

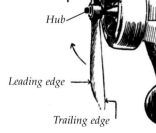

Tip travels farther and faster than hub

Propeller rotates this way

Hub

Leading edge

Trailing edge

PARAGON 1909
The profile of this experimental blade is good but there was no need for such a sweeping shape at the slow spinning speeds of the time.

PITCH AND TWIST
The thrust created by a propeller varies with its speed and the angle at which its blades carve through the air – its pitch. Because the propeller tip spins faster than the hub, the blade is twisted to make the pitch steep near the hub but shallower toward the tip. This keeps thrust even all the way along the blade.

Brass cover to protect the blade from sea spray

LANG 1917
Long and robust, this laminated propeller was made to cope with the power of a 225 hp Sunbeam engine on a Short 184 seaplane. The brass-clad tips protect it from erosion by sea spray.

WOTAN 1917
The laminated construction is clearly visible in this elegant German propeller. The propeller was made by glueing roughly shaped laminations together and then carving them to form a smoothly tapered airfoil.

EXTRA BLADES
As engine power increased, propellers were made with three or four blades to cope with the extra load.

Rivets to hold the brass armor to the blade

Laminations of spruce and ash

Swivel to vary the pitch of the blades

HELE-SHAW-BEACHAM 1928
Ideally, an aircraft needs coarse (steeply) pitched propellers for cruising at speed and fine (shallow) pitch for good thrust at takeoff. So in the late 1920s, many aircraft began using propellers on which the angle of the blades could be changed to suit the conditions. This particular "variable pitch" propeller was operated by engine oil pressure.

FAIREY-REED 1922
As aircraft designers tried to get planes to go faster and faster in the years after World War I, so they demanded thinner blades to slice easily through the air. But thin wooden blades were too weak to take the strain. In 1920, S.A. Reed developed a way of making strong forged aluminium propellers. Over the years, these gradually displaced laminated wooden propellers.

INTEGRALE 1919
The brass sheath covering this wooden-bladed propeller was designed to protect it from enemy attack. Before timing mechanisms were invented (pp. 18-19), propellers on some French fighter planes had even heavier armor-plating to keep them from being destroyed by their own forward-firing machine gun.

Swiveling blade to give the right pitch for both landing and high-speed cruising

UNDUCTED FAN
To save fuel, jet engine manufacturers experimented with propellers called "unducted fans" in the 1980s, but there was no commercial interest in them.

Flying the world

THE TIME BETWEEN THE TWO WORLD WARS was the heroic age of aviation – the age of the first non-stop crossing of the Atlantic, by Alcock and Brown (p.42), Lindbergh's brave solo crossing (p.26) and Kingsford Smith's epic flight over the Pacific in 1928. Feats like these inspired confidence in aviation and, for the first time, planes regularly began to carry passengers. All over the world, new airlines went into business, and more and more people experienced the speed and novelty of flying. Nowhere did air travel grow more than in the USA, where mail contracts helped finance the emerging airlines. Passenger aircraft design made rapid progress here and in 1933 Boeing launched the 247, the world's first modern airliner.

STARS IN THE SKY
Air travel was a new and glamorous experience, and many of the first passengers on the prestigious London-Paris route were American film stars or sports celebrities.

CROYDON AIRPORT
Early airports were often little more than a grass landing strip and a straggle of tents. The world's first modern airport buildings were constructed in Croydon, near London, in 1928.

Flight deck with automatic pilot to reduce stress on the pilot during long flights – a very advanced feature for the 1930s

Metal skin of the plane made strong enough ("stressed") for bracing wires and struts to be unnecessary

THIS IS YOUR CAPTAIN
When the Instone shipping line launched an airline in 1919, its pilots wore the blue uniforms of a ship's captain. This is now standard dress for airline pilots.

Pressure tube for airspeed indicator

BOEING 247D
The Boeing 247D was one of the most advanced planes of its time. It had smooth monoplane wings, a streamlined, all-metal "skin", and landing gear that retracted into the wing during flight. All this helped cut aerodynamic drag so much that the 247D could fly at 180 mph (290 kmh) – faster than most fighter planes. Passengers could be whisked right across the U.S. in under 20 hours.

Front view of Boeing 247D

Boeing 247D in flight with landing gear retracted

De Havilland Dragon

HARDY TRAVELERS
Early passenger planes were tiny in comparison to those of today. The De Havilland Dragon of 1933 (above and right) was one of the smallest, carrying only eight passengers. But even the big Boeing 247D took only ten. Fixed rows of seats became standard only from the 1930s; the first passengers rode in loose wicker armchairs. Even in the 1930s, a long plane journey could be quite an ordeal. Without the pressurized cabins of today (pp. 34-35), airliners tended to fly low and passengers were shaken all over the place by turbulence. If the pilots flew high to avoid the weather, the poor passengers could face bitter cold and altitude sickness.

Passenger cabin of De Havilland Dragon

Highly reliable 550 hp Pratt & Whitney "Wasp" air-cooled radial engine

Variable-pitch propellers (p. 31) to give both high cruising speed and extra power for take-off

Tailplane

FLYING BOAT TO EGYPT
Big flying boats enabled people to fly vast distances to exotic places. Their ability to land on water was vital when airports were few and far between, mechanical breakdown was always a possibility, and long, slow journeys had to be broken by overnight stops.

Monoplane wing good for economy and speed

Aileron

Powerful electric light for night landing

Electric rams to fold landing gear up into the wing after takeoff

IMPERIAL STYLE
The British Handley Page biplanes like this Heracles were the biggest and most luxurious airliners of the 1930s. They were also very safe, flying over two million miles for Imperial Airways without a fatality. But they were slow and old-fashioned compared to the American airliners.

Jetliner

THE JET AIRLINER has transformed air travel since the 1950s. Before then, only the wealthy could afford to fly. Now millions of people travel by air each year. Jetliners are fast and quiet compared with earlier planes. They can also fly high above the weather, carrying passengers smoothly in pressurized cabins that protect them from the reduction in air pressure at high altitudes. On the outside, the jets of today look little different from those of 30 years ago, but beneath the skin, there is a great deal of advanced technology. Sophisticated electronic control and navigation systems have made jetliners much safer to fly in. Airframes now include light, strong carbon-fiber and other composite materials. Computer-designed wings cut fuel costs, and advanced turbofan engines keep (p.36) engine noise to a minimum.

ARMCHAIRS IN THE SKY
The smoothness of the engines, low cabin noise, and high-altitude flying made jetliners very comfortable.

BIT BY BIT
Modern jetliners are built in sections and bolted, riveted, and bonded together with strong adhesive. Because each joint is a weak point, the number of sections is kept to a minimum.

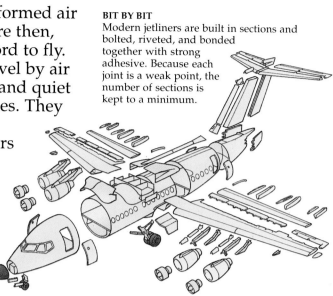

Mounting for wing root, containing central fuel tank

FUSELAGE SECTION
The fuselage tube is the same diameter over most of its length. This makes it cheap and easy to construct, because all the frames and tube pieces are the same size and shape. And if the manufacturer wants to make the plane longer or shorter, all that has to be done is add or take away a fuselage section, or "plug."

Central section of BAe 146 fuselage under construction

Jack placed in landing gear recess to support the fuselage during construction

Green chromate-based anti-corrosion treatment prior to painting

Wing skin made from a single piece of metal for extra strength

Cavity for fuel tank

THE WING
As wing design has improved, the wings of jetliners have become slimmer in comparison to the wings of older airliners (pp. 32-33). This keeps drag to a minimum. Because jetliners cruise at high speeds, their wings also carry complicated flaps and ailerons, for extra lift and control at low speeds for takeoff and landing, and spoiler flaps (air brakes) to slow the plane down quickly after landing.

Engine mounting pylon

Mounting for inner flaps or spoilers, which flip up to slow the plane down after landing

Hydraulic flap control pipe

DE HAVILLAND COMET

The Comet, the world's first jetliner, came into commercial service in 1952 – and at once halved international flight times. But a few early Comets had tragic crashes, and it was with the Boeing 707 of 1958 and the Douglas DC-8 that the age of jet travel really began.

JUMBO JET

When the huge Boeing 747, the first wide-bodied jet, entered service in 1970, many airline experts wondered whether enough passengers could ever be found to fly in it. In fact, the jumbo jet helped make air travel affordable, for the first time, for billions of people.

INSIDE THE FUSELAGE

The structure of a jetliner needs to be immensely strong to withstand the stresses of high-speed flight and the constant strain of pressurization and depressurization. Any weaknesses could be disastrous. So the strength and durability of every little section are carefully assessed – an enormous task that once involved scores of "stressmen" but is now made much easier by computers. Yet strength alone is not enough. The structure must be light, too, which is why aluminum alloy is used extensively. There are hoop frames and stringers all the way down the inside of the fuselage, but these are small and much of the fuselage's strength comes from the metal tube "skin." This makes the structure both light and strong.

Light alloy hoop frame, machined from a single piece of metal for strength

Brackets for overhead luggage lockers

Soundproofing insulation

Passenger compartment floor

Electric control wires

Hydraulic control pipes

Stringers bonded along the fuselage skin for extra strength

Aluminum alloy skin

Luggage hold

Inside a fuselage section of the BAe 146

BAe 146 seat plan

SITTING TIGHT

To keep costs down, modern airliners squeeze in as many passenger seats as possible, but seat spacing varies according to the class of travel and whether the plane is for long-haul or short-haul flights.

Mounting for "roll spoiler" flap to stabilize the plane during banking

Mounting point for large flaps that extend out and down behind the wing for low-speed flight

Aileron

Rear view of the right wing of the BAe 146 under construction

COMPLETED JETLINER

The BAe 146 is a modern, medium-size jetliner, powered by high bypass turbofan engines for quietness and economy.

Jet propulsion

THE BIRTH OF THE JET ENGINE in the late 1930s marked a revolution in aviation. Some very highly tuned piston-engined planes were then flying at speeds in excess of 440 mph (700 kmh) – but only by burning a great deal of fuel. Jet engines made speeds like this so easy to achieve that, by the early 1960s, even big airliners on scheduled services were flying faster – and some military jets could streak along at 1,500 mph (2,500 kmh), more than twice the speed of sound. Now, almost all airliners, most military planes, and many small business planes ("executive jets") are powered by one of the several different kinds of jet engine. With the exception of Concorde, supersonic flight has proved too noisy and expensive for airliners, but jet engine technology is still making steady progress.

PIONEER JET
The first prototype jet engines were built at the same time by Pabst von Ohain in Germany and Frank Whittle in Britain – although neither knew of the other's work. Whittle's engine was first used in the Gloster E28/39 of 1941 (above).

BREAKING THE SOUND BARRIER
In 1947, in the specially built Bell X-1 rocket plane, test pilot Chuck Yeager succeeded in flying faster than sound – about 700 mph (1,100 kmh).

Turbine power

Jet engines should really be called "gas turbines". Like piston engines, their power comes from burning fuel. The difference is that they burn fuel continuously to spin the blades of a turbine rather than intermittently to push on a piston. In a turbojet, the turbine simply turns the compressor. In a turbofan, it drives the big fan at the front as well.

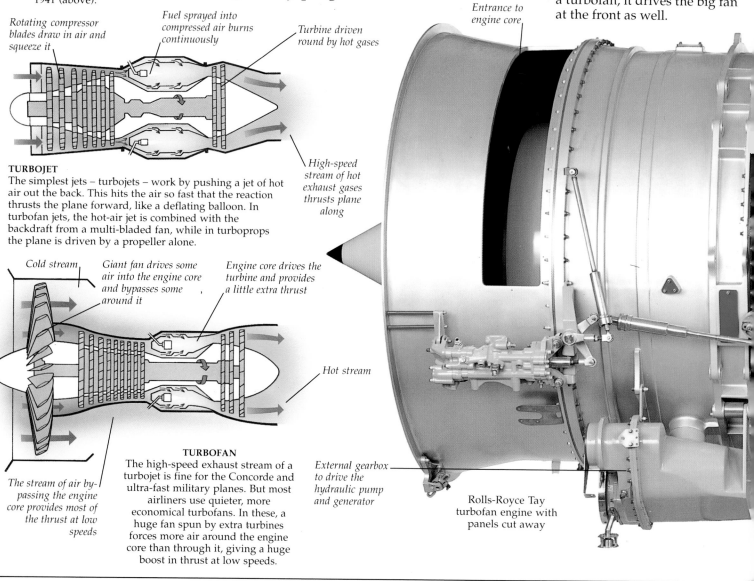

Rotating compressor blades draw in air and squeeze it

Fuel sprayed into compressed air burns continuously

Turbine driven round by hot gases

Entrance to engine core

TURBOJET
The simplest jets – turbojets – work by pushing a jet of hot air out the back. This hits the air so fast that the reaction thrusts the plane forward, like a deflating balloon. In turbofan jets, the hot-air jet is combined with the backdraft from a multi-bladed fan, while in turboprops the plane is driven by a propeller alone.

High-speed stream of hot exhaust gases thrusts plane along

Cold stream

Giant fan drives some air into the engine core and bypasses some around it

Engine core drives the turbine and provides a little extra thrust

Hot stream

The stream of air by-passing the engine core provides most of the thrust at low speeds

TURBOFAN
The high-speed exhaust stream of a turbojet is fine for the Concorde and ultra-fast military planes. But most airliners use quieter, more economical turbofans. In these, a huge fan spun by extra turbines forces more air around the engine core than through it, giving a huge boost in thrust at low speeds.

External gearbox to drive the hydraulic pump and generator

Rolls-Royce Tay turbofan engine with panels cut away

Front-view of
Rolls-Royce Tay

*Titanium fan
blades*

Rear view of
Rolls-Royce Tay

*Exit for hot
stream from
engine core*

*Exit for cold
stream bypass*

*Exhaust
nozzles*

POWER FAN
Modern turbofan engines owe much of their immense
power to the giant fan at the front, and the design of
the fan blades has a critical effect on fuel economy. In
the Rolls-Royce Tay, the fan pushes more than three
times as much air through the bypass duct to provide
propulsion as through the engine core. In earlier
turbofans, the proportions were about equal.

BLOWING HOT AND COLD
Most of the turbofan's propulsive power is
provided by the "cold-stream" air rushing
through the bypass duct. The faster, "hot-stream"
gas from the engine shoots out through the lobed
exhaust nozzles. The lobes help mix the hot and
cold streams quickly and reduce noise.

*Combustion
chamber where
fuel spray burns
continuously in
the compressed
air*

*Bypass casing made of
carbon fiber and plastic
honeycomb for lightness
and sound insulation*

*Turbines made
of exotic metal
alloys to
withstand
running red
hot all the time*

BEYOND SOUND
The Concorde, the
only successful
supersonic airliner,
flies the Atlantic
twice as fast as
conventional jets. But
its turbojet engines
can be noisy.

*Rows of rotating
compressor blades drive air
through the engine,
compressing the air as it
passes through*

Landing gear

T HE FIRST AIRPLANES landed on wheels borrowed from
motorcycles and cars and mounted on wooden or metal struts.
They did the job, but the shock of a poor landing was often
enough to make the struts collapse. Soon the landing gear,
or "undercarriage," was given basic springs to cushion the
blow, and special aviation wheels were designed. But as
planes grew heavier and landing and takeoff speeds rose,
wooden struts and wire wheels gave way to pressed-steel
wheels and strong hydraulic (fluid-filled) shock absorbers.
Wheels were also mounted further apart on the wings for
extra stability. From the 1940s on, wheels on all but the
smallest, slowest planes were folded up into the wings in
flight to cut down air resistance. With the coming of the jet age
after World War II, the demands on landing gear increased
still further. Innovations such as disk and anti-lock brakes,
later adopted on cars, were first tried on airplanes. Modern
jetliner landing gear is highly sophisticated, with elaborate
suspension and braking systems designed to support the full
force of a 150-ton plane landing at 125 mph (200 kmh) or
more and bring it quickly and safely to a halt.

LANDING ON WATER
In the days when good landing strips were few
and far between, it made sense to land on water.
On seaplanes, a step two-thirds along the
underside of the float helped it "plane" on the
water like a speedboat. This cut water drag
enough for the aircraft to reach takeoff speed.

LIGHTLY SPOKED
There were no brakes on this wheel from a
pre-World War I plane. So it did not need
elaborate criss-crossed spokes to resist
braking forces.

*Wooden
landing
strut*

*Skids to keep the
plane from
tipping forward
when landing on
soft ground*

*Elasticated
rubber shock
absorbers*

SPRUNG TAIL SKID
The rear ends of the
pioneers' planes were so
light, there was no need
for a wheel; a simple skid
was enough.

COMING DOWN GENTLY
The 1909 Deperdussin came down
so lightly and slowly that elastic
rubber straps made fairly effective
landing springs. Curved skids on
the front helped to keep the plane
from pitching forward when
landing on soft ground – a
common hazard in the early days.

LANDING LIGHT

As landing speeds rose sharply with the coming of jets in the 1950s, ever-longer paved runways had to be built for jetliners to land on safely. Bigger aircraft also switched from a single wheel to multi-wheel "bogie" landing legs. Bogies were not only smaller and lighter, but also spread the landing load over a wider area – and reduced the danger from a burst tire. At the same time, most planes acquired wheels under the nose. Nose wheels meant that planes could land level and, in effect, drive onto the runway like a car. Before nose wheels, pilots had to skilfully stall (pp. 40-41) the plane just above the ground, letting the main and tail wheels drop onto the runway at the same time.

UP AND UNDER

In the bid for speed, World War II fighters like the Spitfire (above) pioneered simple mechanisms for folding the wheels right up into the wings in flight.

Hydraulic disk-brake pipes

SPITFIRE WHEEL

Light and robust cast-alloy wheels, now common on cars, were used on aircraft like the Spitfire many years before they were tried on cars.

Hydraulic spring and damper to soften landing

Hydraulic ram slides up inside main leg to absorb landing shocks

Auxiliary shock absorber

Swivel joints to allow for spring compression

STEEL WHEEL

Pressed-steel wheels provided the extra strength needed for the faster, heavier planes of the 1920s. This one is from a Hawker Hart similar to that on page 24.

TWO BIG WHEELS

The big monoplane airliners and bombers of the 1930s and 40s had one huge retracting wheel on each wing. On this 1930s Armstrong Whitworth airliner, the rear landing leg folded in the middle so that a hydraulic jack could lift the wheel back up into the engine housing in flight.

Bogie with four twin-tired wheels

Tire designed to stand enormous loads and huge heat buildup on landing

Landing leg from 1950s Avro Vulcan bomber

Controlling the plane

A CAR OR A BOAT can be steered only to the left or right, but an airplane can be controlled in three dimensions. It can "pitch" nose-up or nose-down to climb or dive. It can "roll" from side to side, dipping one wing or the other. And it can "yaw" to the left or to the right, like a car steering. For many in-flight maneuvers the pilot has to use not just one control, but all three simultaneously – which is why flying demands good coordination. Indeed, all the time the plane is in the air, the pilot must constantly trim the controls simply to keep the plane flying straight and level – for even on the calmest day, there is air turbulence to tip it off balance. "Automatic pilots" compensate for such upsets and make life for the pilot much easier.

CONTROL COLUMN
As early as 1909, Blériot and other French aviation pioneers had devised a single lever, or lever and wheel, to control pitch and roll. This operates the wing ailerons and the tailplane elevators via cables.

RUDDER BAR
Yaw is controlled by pushing on the rudder bar with either the left or the right foot to swing the rudder left or right.

THE STALL
If a plane flies too slowly, airflow over the wings may not give enough lift. It then "stalls," pitching downward, and may go into a spin. With enough height, a skilled pilot can usually recover.

Nose comes up

Main wing meets the air at a sharper angle, increasing lift

Elevators raised, pushing down the tail

PITCHING UP
Pulling the control column back raises the elevators. If the aircraft is flying level, the nose rises and the plane pitches upward. Since the wing now meets the air at a greater angle, giving more lift, it will start to climb, providing engine power is increased.

Elevator flat, keeping the plane level

LEVEL FLIGHT
In level flight, the tail helps to keep the aircraft steady, like the feathers on a dart. If the aircraft is pitched up or down by turbulence, the tailplane helps it level out again.

Elevators lowered, increasing tail lift

Nose dips

Main wing meets the air at a shallower angle, reducing lift and drag

PITCHING DOWN
Lowering the elevators, by pushing the control column forward, makes the tailplane lift. This pitches the nose downward and the aircraft will gather speed as it descends. To keep speed down for a normal landing, the pilot throttles back at the same time to reduce power.

ROLLING LEFT

To roll to the left, the pilot pushes the control column over to the left. This raises the aileron on the left wing, reducing lift, and lowers the aileron on the right wing, increasing lift.

Left aileron raised, reducing lift on left wing

Right aileron lowered, increasing lift on right wing

ROLLING RIGHT

To roll to the right, the pilot pushes the control column to the right, raising the right aileron and lowering the left aileron. If the ailerons are kept deflected, the plane will roll farther and farther and eventually roll right over. So once the plane is rolled at the right angle, the pilot must straighten the column again.

Left aileron lowered, increasing lift on left wing

Right aileron raised, reducing lift on right wing

TURNING LEFT

While moving on the ground, pushing with the left foot on the rudder bar will swing the rudder over to the left and make the plane yaw around the same way. But a plane cannot be turned like this in the air. Instead, it has to be banked around – like cornering on a bicycle. To make a banked turn, the pilot has to yaw and roll the plane at the same time. Banking for a left turn means pushing the control column to the left while pressing on the rudder with the left foot.

Rudder swung left, yawing the plane to the left

Rudder swung right, yawing the plane to the right

TURNING RIGHT

Banking for a right turn means pressing on the rudder bar with the right foot while pushing the control column over to the right at the same time. Balancing the rudder and control column movement to achieve just the right bank angle requires skill and experience.

AERIAL TWISTS

Almost from the first, pilots started trying new maneuvers, and in many air forces, aerobatics is part of routine training. In the 1920s, Flying Circuses thrilled audiences all over the world with breathtaking aerobatic displays in agile biplanes.

In the cockpit

ENCLOSED COCKPITS had to await the development of safety glass in the late 1920s. Until then, pilots sat in the open, exposed to howling winds, freezing cold, and damp – with nothing more to protect them than a tiny windshield and warm clothes. Naturally, comfort was a low priority in these open cockpits, and they were very basic and functional in appearance. There were few instruments, and engine gauges were just as often on the engine itself as in the cockpit. The layout of the main flight controls became established fairly early on, with a rudder bar at the pilot's feet for turning and a control column, or "joy stick," between the knees for diving, climbing, and banking. Some early planes had a wheel rather than a joy stick but it served the same purpose. This basic layout is still used in light planes today.

DEPERDUSSIN 1909
The cockpits of the earliest planes were very simple, for they had no instruments. With a large fuel tank obscuring the view ahead, the pilot had to constantly lean out of the cockpit to check height and attitude.

VICKERS VIMY 1919
The Vimy was designed toward the end of World War I for long-range British bombing raids over industrial targets in Germany, and the cockpit was laid out accordingly, with two seats - one for the pilot and one for the observer. The pilot had to read engine speed and oil pressure from gauges mounted on the engines themselves.

Hand-wound magneto to provide electric current for starting

Instrument light switches

Clock

Altimeter to show height

ATLANTIC FLIGHT *above*
The Vimy was the plane in which John Alcock and Arthur Brown made the first nonstop flight over the Atlantic on June 14-15 1919, enduring 16 hours of freezing fog and drizzle in an open cockpit.

Inclinometers to show bank and pitch

Compass

Engine radiator shutter control

Rudder bar

Control wheel turned to bank left or right

Engine throttle and fuel mixture control

TIGER MOTH

By the 1930s, the joy stick had become the standard form of control and even the simplest planes, like this De Havilland Tiger Moth, had a range of basic instruments: airspeed indicator, altimeter, turn indicator, compass, engine rev counter, and oil pressure gauge. But there was still no artificial horizon, to help the pilot keep the plane level, so the plane could be flown only in clear weather when the horizon was visible. The whole cockpit was functional and basic, with none of the comforts light planes usually have today, such as carpets, molded seats, and heaters.

Turn indicator

Small windshield

Notice saying that aerobatic maneuvers may be performed

Engine rev counter

Compass

Airspeed indicator

Altimeter

Joy stick

Lever to close landing/takeoff slats on the wing during aerobatic maneuvers

SKY TIGER

The DH Tiger Moth biplane was one of the most popular of all light planes in the 1930s. Simple and reliable, it was used for everything from training and crop spraying to daring aerobatic displays.

Notice reminding the pilot that the plane can cruise at 94 mph (150 kmh) but will stall if flown slower than 45 mph (72 kmh)

Engine oil pressure gauge

Rudder bar

Throttle

On the flight deck

THE FLIGHT DECK OF A MODERN JETLINER looks dauntingly complicated with its array of switches, dials, and displays for such things as engine condition, hydraulics, navigational aid, and so on, not to mention the basic flight controls. Increasingly, computers are taking over certain functions, and what was once a mass of dials has been replaced by neat screens on which the pilot can change the information displayed at the flick of a switch.

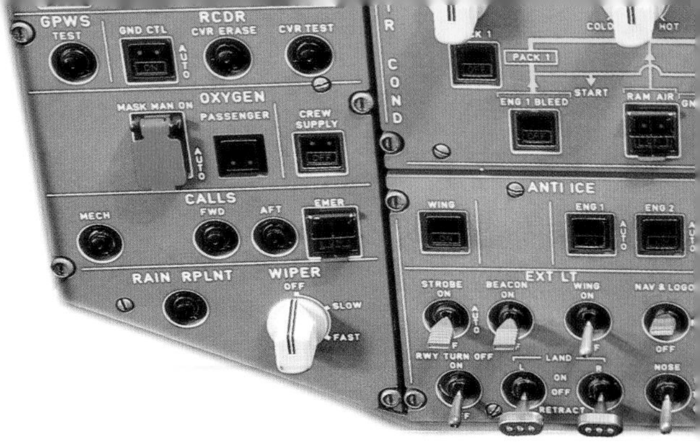

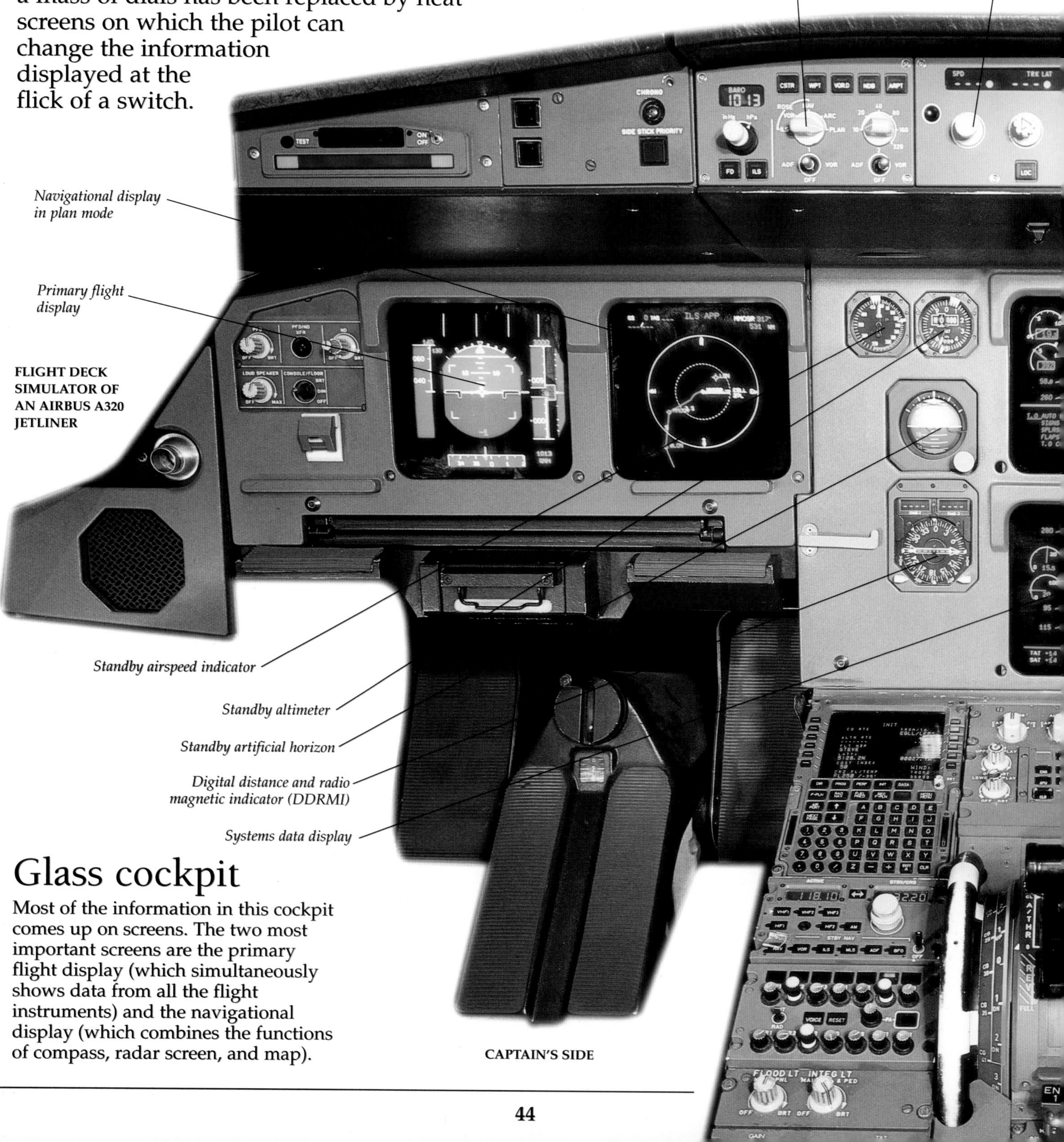

Navigation display mode selector

Mach (airspeed) selector

Navigational display in plan mode

Primary flight display

FLIGHT DECK SIMULATOR OF AN AIRBUS A320 JETLINER

Standby airspeed indicator

Standby altimeter

Standby artificial horizon

Digital distance and radio magnetic indicator (DDRMI)

Systems data display

Glass cockpit

Most of the information in this cockpit comes up on screens. The two most important screens are the primary flight display (which simultaneously shows data from all the flight instruments) and the navigational display (which combines the functions of compass, radar screen, and map).

CAPTAIN'S SIDE

44

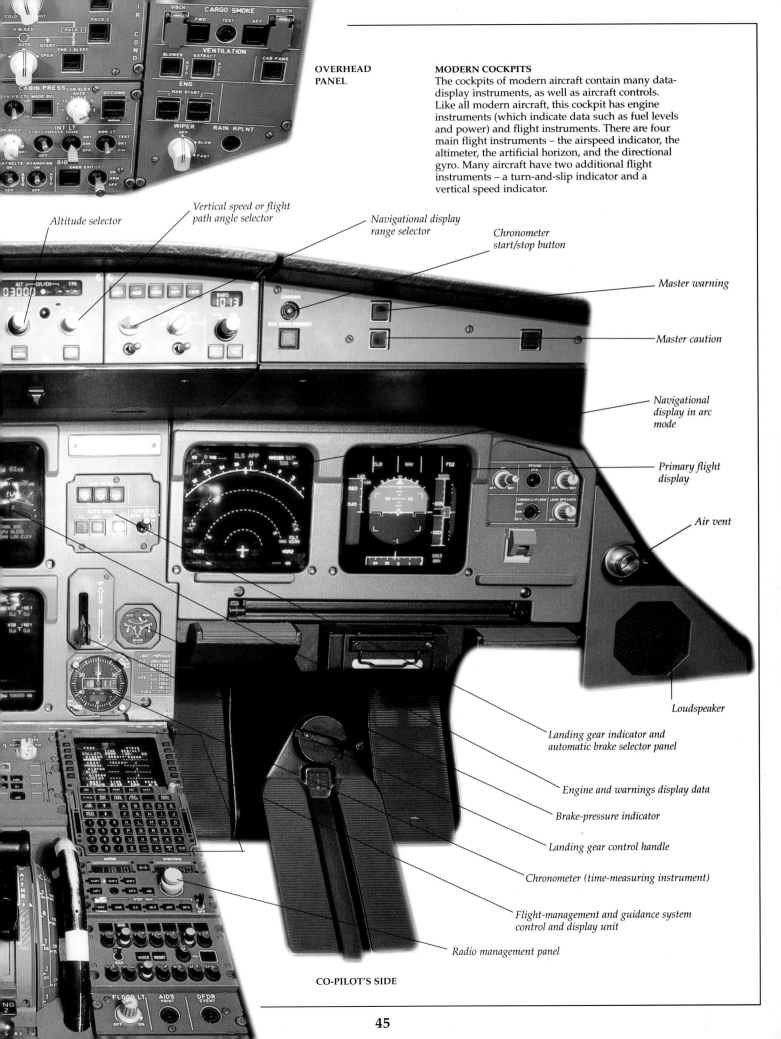

MODERN COCKPITS
The cockpits of modern aircraft contain many data-display instruments, as well as aircraft controls. Like all modern aircraft, this cockpit has engine instruments (which indicate data such as fuel levels and power) and flight instruments. There are four main flight instruments – the airspeed indicator, the altimeter, the artificial horizon, and the directional gyro. Many aircraft have two additional flight instruments – a turn-and-slip indicator and a vertical speed indicator.

Altitude selector

Vertical speed or flight path angle selector

Navigational display range selector

Chronometer start/stop button

Master warning

Master caution

Navigational display in arc mode

Primary flight display

Air vent

Loudspeaker

Landing gear indicator and automatic brake selector panel

Engine and warnings display data

Brake-pressure indicator

Landing gear control handle

Chronometer (time-measuring instrument)

Flight-management and guidance system control and display unit

Radio management panel

CO-PILOT'S SIDE

Flying instruments

Pressure plate

Spring

THE WRIGHT BROTHERS (p. 14) flew with nothing more in the way of instruments than an engine rev counter, a stopwatch, and a wind meter to tell them roughly how fast the plane was going. But the dangers of stalling by flying too slow (pp. 40-41) soon made it clear that every flying machine should have an accurate airspeed indicator as standard. As aircraft began to fly higher and farther, an altimeter to indicate height and a magnetic compass to help keep a straight course were quickly added as well. Yet for a long time, pilots flew "by the seat of their pants," judging the plane's attitude by feel alone when they could not see. It was only with Elmer Sperry's development of gyroscope-stabilized instruments in 1929 that pilots were given a bank-and-turn indicator and an artificial horizon. Gyroscopes – a kind of spinning top that stays level no matter what angle the plane is at – enabled pilots to "fly on instruments" when visibility was poor.

DOUBLE TUBE
This is one of the first instruments to give a continuous and reliable indication of airspeed. It works by comparing static pressure (ordinary air pressure) to dynamic pressure (from the plane pushing forward). Its twin pipes point into the airflow, one running straight through but the other ending in a perforated cylinder. The pressure difference between the two, measured by a flexible diaphragm, indicates the airspeed.

HOW FAST?
Among the earliest speed indicators were anemometers (wind meters) adapted from weather forecasting. The pilot got a rough idea of how fast the plane was going by timing so many seconds on a stopwatch while noting on the meter dials how many times the airflow turned the fan on the front.

Farnborough airspeed indicator c. 1909

Diaphragm

Static pipe

Dynamic pipe

Static tube

Pitot head

Dynamic tube

PITOT HEAD
The twin-tube pressure method pioneered by Farnborough soon became the basis for measuring airspeed on all aircraft. The twin tube was refined into the pressure-sensing pitot head mounted on the airframe. Rubber tubes connected the pitot to the airspeed gauge in the cockpit.

Connecting tube

Gauge

Ogilvie airspeed indicator c. 1918

MACHMETER
As jet planes approached and even exceeded the speed of sound in the 1950s, they were given mach meters. These showed how fast the plane was flying relative to the speed of sound.

SPEED LIMIT
In the years after World War II, airspeed indicators often had a pointer (arrow) showing the maximum safe speed of the plane.

WING SPRING
This dates from 1910, but even in the 1930s some planes still used these simple devices. They showed airspeed according to how far the pressure plate was forced back against a spring by the airflow.

HOW STRAIGHT?
In this bank-and-turn indicator, a simple alcohol level indicates how much the plane is banked. Changes in direction are shown by the upper turn needle, linked to an electrically driven gyroscope.

WHICH WAY?
Landing in poor weather was made much safer by this gyroscopic instrument. It helped the pilot maintain a course and glide slope set by a radio beam lined up with the runway.

With the sighting string below the horizon, the plane is diving

With the sighting string above the horizon, the plane is climbing

HOW HIGH?
To tell how high they were, the pioneer aviators used to whip from their pockets little altimeters such as the Elliott (below) – similar to those used by mountaineers for years before. But the aerial antics of World War I fighters showed the need for a big dial fixed to the panel (left).

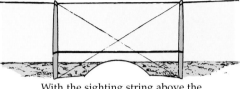

With the sighting string dipping left below the horizon, the plane is rolling left

HOW LEVEL?
In the early days, pilots could only look at the horizon, perhaps with the aid of a "sighting string" (above right), to tell them how much their machine was pitching or rolling. At night or in thick cloud, the pilot would soon be completely disoriented. Research showed that even the most experienced pilot could not fly "blind" for more than eight minutes without getting into a spin. The answer was a gyroscopic artificial horizon.

Inside the black box

All modern airliners and military planes now carry a "black box" or "flight data recorder" to give a complete history of the flight in case of an accident. The box is connected to all the aircraft's main systems and records everything that happens during the flight, monitoring flight deck instruments, engine data, and even all that the crew says.

Kevlar lining to insulate the recorder against the heat of a fire

Recorder motor

BOXED IN
All the data in this box are stored in eight tracks on a magnetic tape. An enormously strong, well-insulated. titanium alloy case protects the tape against crash damage and fire.

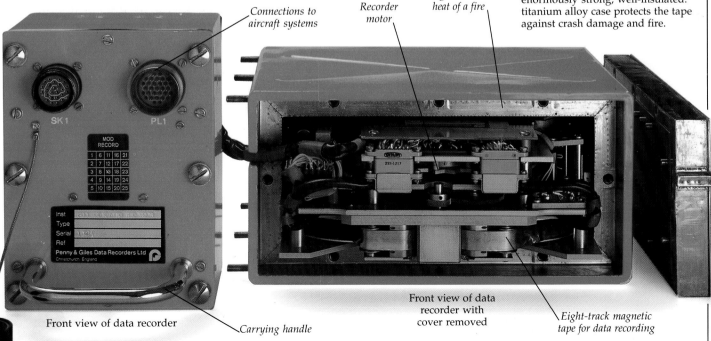

Connections to aircraft systems

Front view of data recorder

Carrying handle

Front view of data recorder with cover removed

Eight-track magnetic tape for data recording

Rotating wings

THE IDEA OF FLYING on rotating wings is old. As long ago as 1400, European children played with flying toys with whirring blades. Indeed, up until the Wright brothers' *Flyer*, many felt the future of flight lay with rotating rather than fixed wings. Spinning wings, they knew, would slice through the air to provide lift just like fixed wings (p. 11). But while a fixed-wing plane must keep moving, a rotating-wing plane could hover in one place. In the early 1900s, many whirling-wing contraptions did lift some way off the ground. Yet the chances of controlled flight seemed remote until Juan de la Cierva created the autogiro.

Rotor blade

LOOK! NO WINGS
The autogiro was never meant to be a helicopter, but a plane without wings – a plane that was much safer than fixed-wing planes because it would not stall simply by flying too slow. Indeed, Cierva's first autogiros did have stubby wings to assist takeoff (right). Publicity for the autogiro always emphasized how it could drift safely to the ground, "slower than a parachute," in case of engine failure.

Autogiro

In early helicopter experiments, inventors had used ever more powerful engines to get their machines to rise. Cierva's stroke of genius was to see that rotating wings can provide lift without the engine. Like a maple seed pod whirling gently down to Earth, a freely rotating wing continues to spin by itself when moving through the air, pushed around by the pressure of air on the underside of the wings. Cierva called this "self-rotation" or "autogiro."

K4232

CIERVA C-30
The C-30 was the most successful of all autogiros made in the 1930s. This example was one of many sold to the military for observation and for use as markers to set up radar in World War II.

Unique upswept tailplane with normal camber on this side only to counterbalance the rotation of the blades

Fabric-covered tube-steel fuselage similar to that of a biplane

Steerable tail-wheel

CARS OF THE SKY
For a while in the 1930s, many believed that autogiros would be the Model T Fords of the air – aircraft for everyone which would do away with traffic jams once and for all. Ads for Pitcairn Aviation, which made autogiros in the U.S., were aimed clearly at the fashionable set. What could be simpler, they suggested, than to jump into the autogiro on your front lawn and drop in at your country club for a quick game of golf?

PIVOTING BLADES
Primitive rotor craft tended to roll over because the advancing blade cut through the air faster than the receding one, and so was lifted more. Cierva solved this problem with hinges that allowed the advancing blade to rise without affecting the plane.

Blade lift hinges

Sideways drag hinges and shock absorbers allow the blades to advance or trail slightly as they rotate to reduce stress on root of blade

Hanging control column allows the pilot to tilt the blades in any direction

Drive from the engine to start the rotors spinning for takeoff

SNAIL'S FLIGHT
To demonstrate its safety potential, the C-30 used to fly into the wind so slowly it could be outpaced by a runner.

Rotor blade construction, showing how similar the profile is to conventional wings

150 hp Armstrong Siddeley seven-cylinder radial engine

Conventional propeller to pull the aircraft forward for takeoff and normal flight

Oil-filled shock absorbers for softer landing

49

Helicopter

OF ALL FLYING MACHINES, none is quite so versatile as the helicopter. Its whirling rotor blades enable it to shoot straight up in the air, hover for minute after minute over the same spot, and land on an area little bigger than a bus. It burns up fuel at a frightening rate because the engine, via the rotors, provides all the lifting force. It also takes great skill to fly, for the pilot has three flight controls to handle - rudder, "collective pitch," and "cyclic pitch" - one more than conventional aircraft (pp. 40-41). But it has proved its worth in many situations, from traffic monitoring to dramatic rescues.

SPINNING DREAMS
Helicopters have a long history, but many early experimenters were regarded as nutcases. Perhaps some of them were.

Rotor blades

How a helicopter flies

A helicopter's rotor blades are really long, thin wings. The engine spins them around so that they cut through the air just like a conventional wing (p. 11). In a way, the rotor is also like a huge propeller, hauling the helicopter upward just like the propeller pulls a plane along (p. 30).

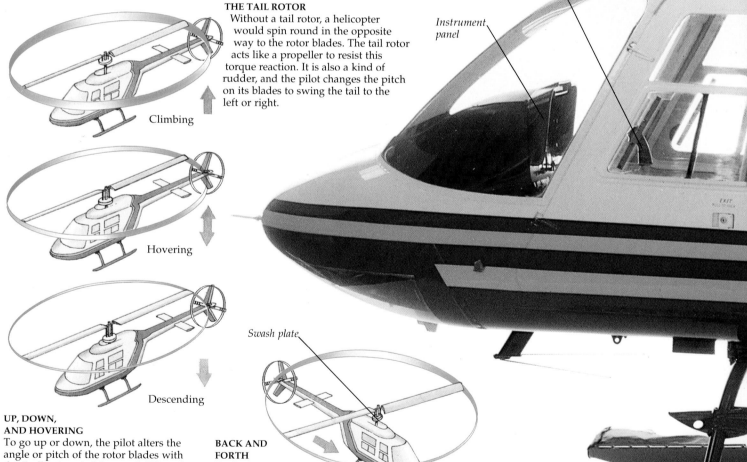

Pitch controls

Instrument panel

THE TAIL ROTOR
Without a tail rotor, a helicopter would spin round in the opposite way to the rotor blades. The tail rotor acts like a propeller to resist this torque reaction. It is also a kind of rudder, and the pilot changes the pitch on its blades to swing the tail to the left or right.

Climbing

Hovering

Descending

Swash plate

UP, DOWN, AND HOVERING
To go up or down, the pilot alters the angle or pitch of the rotor blades with the "collective pitch" control. When the blades are almost flat, they give no lift and the helicopter sinks. To climb, the pilot steepens the pitch of the blades, increasing lift. To hover, however, the pilot sets the blades at a precise angle in between. It all works through a sliding collar on the rotor shaft called the swash plate which pushes up or pulls down on rods linked to the blades.

BACK AND FORTH
To fly forward or backward, or bank for a turn, the pilot tilts the whole rotor with the "cyclic pitch" control. This tilts the swash plate so that the pitch of each blade varies in turn as it goes around. At the point where the plate is lowest, pitch is shallow and lift is limited. Straight opposite, however, the plate is at its highest and a steep pitch gives a lot of lift. The effect is to tilt the whole rotor over in the way the pilot wants to go, pulling the helicopter with it.

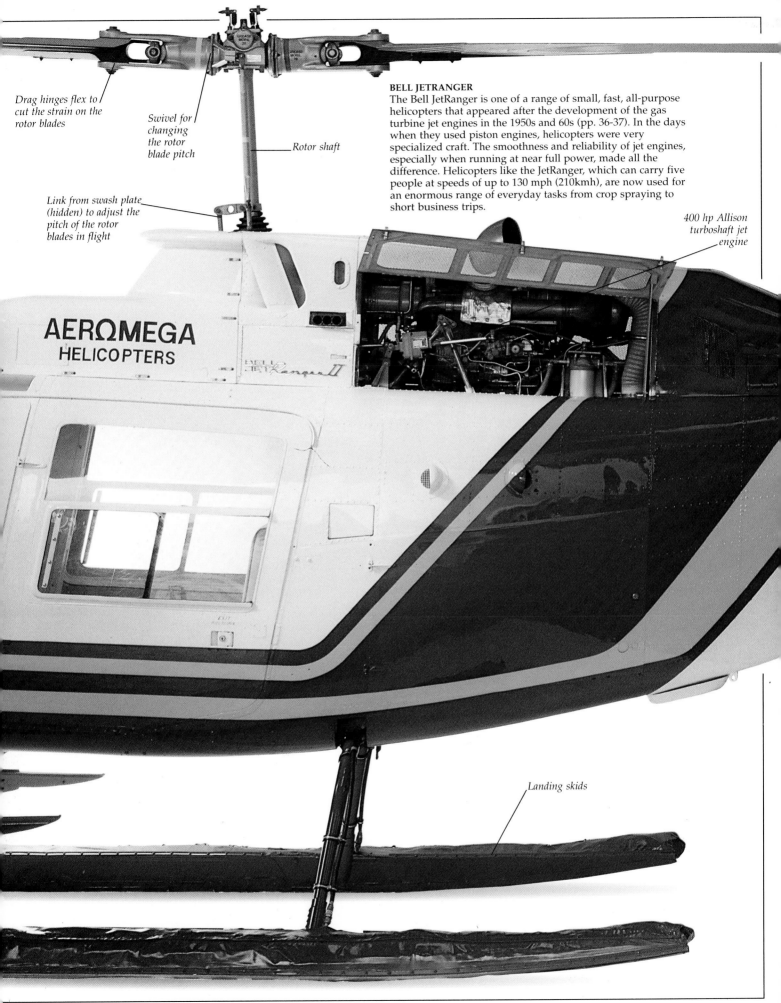

Drag hinges flex to
cut the strain on the
rotor blades

Swivel for
changing
the rotor
blade pitch

Rotor shaft

Link from swash plate
(hidden) to adjust the
pitch of the rotor
blades in flight

BELL JETRANGER
The Bell JetRanger is one of a range of small, fast, all-purpose
helicopters that appeared after the development of the gas
turbine jet engines in the 1950s and 60s (pp. 36-37). In the days
when they used piston engines, helicopters were very
specialized craft. The smoothness and reliability of jet engines,
especially when running at near full power, made all the
difference. Helicopters like the JetRanger, which can carry five
people at speeds of up to 130 mph (210kmh), are now used for
an enormous range of everyday tasks from crop spraying to
short business trips.

400 hp Allison
turboshaft jet
engine

AERΩMEGA
HELICOPTERS

Landing skids

Continued on next page

CLIPPER OF THE CLOUDS
The idea of rotary-wing flight fired the imagination of many creative minds in the 19th century. The flying helicopter toys of Sir George Cayley (p. 10) were famous, but many other people built working models. These models did little more than climb up erratically into the air then drop. But the visionary French inventor Gabriel de la Landelle was convinced that one day machines like the tall-masted Steam Airliner he drew in 1863 (left) would sail majestically through the skies.

THE FIRST HELICOPTER FLIGHT?
Even in the early 20th century, many believed helicopters might still beat fixed wing planes into the air. They were wrong. Yet in 1907, just four years after the Wright brothers' first flight, this primitive tandem-rotor helicopter, built by French mechanic Paul Cornu, lifted him off the ground, if only for 20 seconds.

G-HUMT

Stabilizers to prevent boom from swinging up or down

Boom

Swash plate

Rotor blade pitch control rods

Leading edge of rotor blade

Pilot's seat

Engine housing

THE BIRTH OF THE HELICOPTER
Despite the early success of pioneers like Cornu, it proved immensely difficult to build a stable, controllable helicopter. The breakthrough came only with the invention of the autogiro (pp. 48-49), which taught how control could be achieved by altering the "pitch" (angle) of the rotor blades. In 1937, German designer Heinrich Focke built a craft with an airplane fuselage and two huge rotors instead of wings. It could fly up and down, backward and forward, and even hover. Within months another German, Anton Flettner, had built the first true helicopter – a nimble machine with two big blades that meshed like a cake whisk. Focke and Flettner used two rotors (turning in opposite directions) to prevent torque reaction (p. 50). But in 1939, Igor Sikorsky came up with the much simpler tail-rotor, and in his experimental VS-300 (above) pioneered the design that has been used for helicopters ever since.

Gearbox

BUTTERFLY WINGS
The rubber-band-powered helicopter toys made by Alphonse Pénaud and Dandrieux in the 1870s were the inspiration for many rotary-wing enthusiasts.

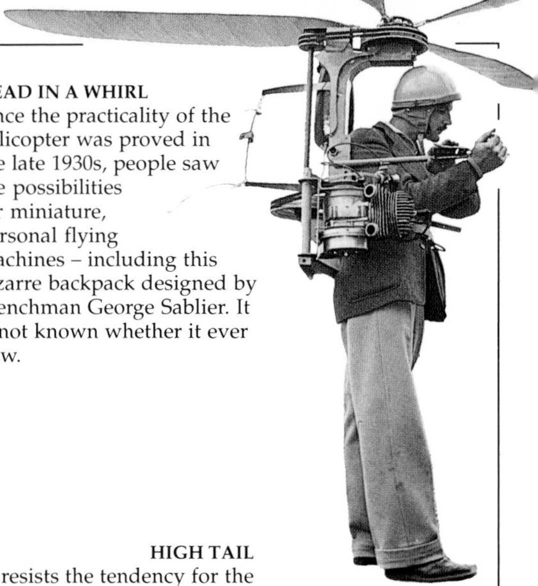

Tail fin

Tail rotor

HEAD IN A WHIRL
Once the practicality of the helicopter was proved in the late 1930s, people saw the possibilities for miniature, personal flying machines – including this bizarre backpack designed by Frenchman George Sablier. It is not known whether it ever flew.

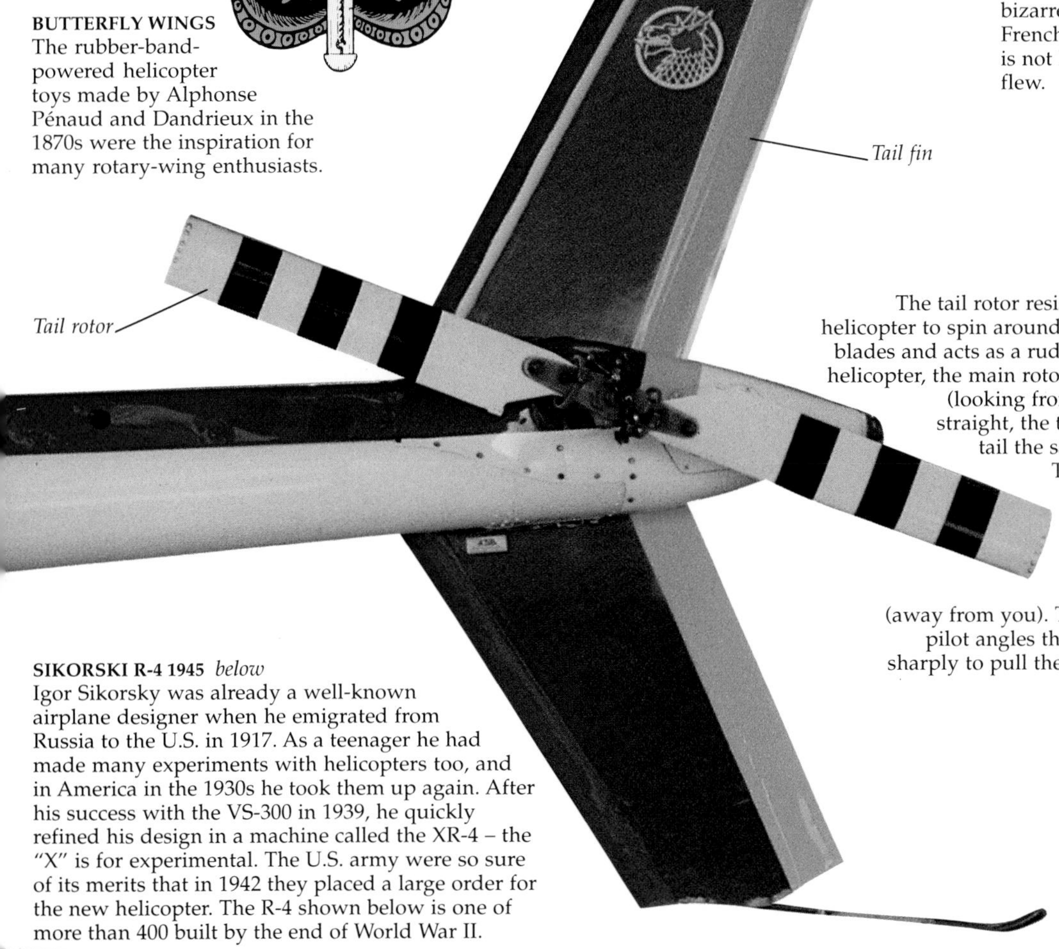

HIGH TAIL
The tail rotor resists the tendency for the helicopter to spin around in reaction to the rotor blades and acts as a rudder (p. 50). On this Bell helicopter, the main rotor blades turn clockwise (looking from above). So, to keep it straight, the tail rotor must push the tail the same way (toward you). To steer it to the left, the pilot flattens the tail rotor blades so that they push weakly and allow the tail to swing counterclockwise (away from you). To steer to the right, the pilot angles the tail rotor blades more sharply to pull the tail strongly clockwise (toward you).

SIKORSKI R-4 1945 *below*
Igor Sikorsky was already a well-known airplane designer when he emigrated from Russia to the U.S. in 1917. As a teenager he had made many experiments with helicopters too, and in America in the 1930s he took them up again. After his success with the VS-300 in 1939, he quickly refined his design in a machine called the XR-4 – the "X" is for experimental. The U.S. army were so sure of its merits that in 1942 they placed a large order for the new helicopter. The R-4 shown below is one of more than 400 built by the end of World War II.

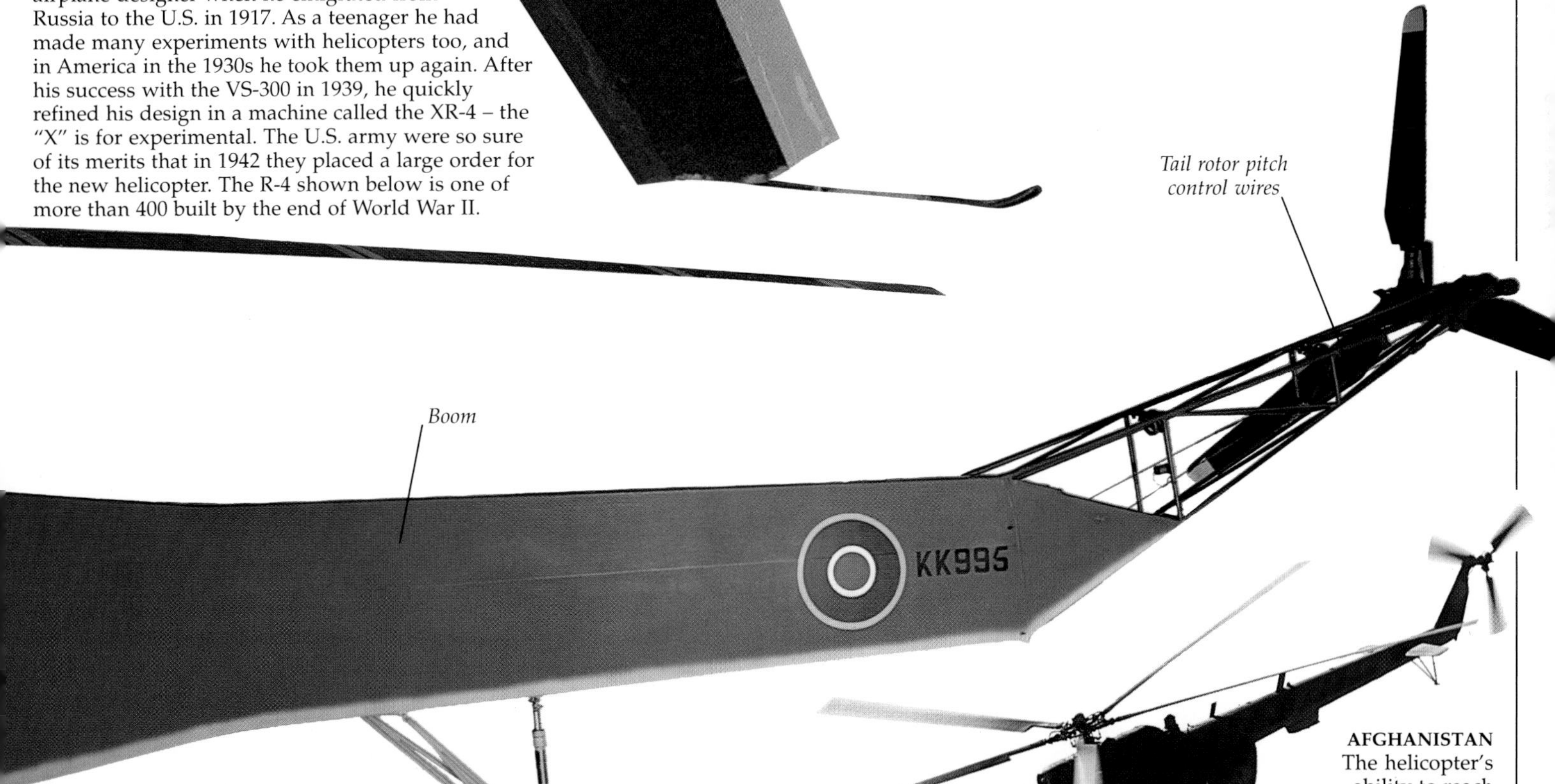

Tail rotor pitch control wires

Boom

KK995

Rear landing wheel

AFGHANISTAN
The helicopter's ability to reach inaccessible places is invaluable in war.

Hot-air balloon

As a sport, ballooning all but died out after World War I – mainly because the gas needed had become too difficult and expensive to obtain. Then in the 1960s, Ed Yost, Tracy Barnes and others in the U.S. started to experiment with balloons inflated with hot air, just like the Montgolfier brothers' balloon nearly 200 years earlier. What was new about their balloons was that the envelopes were made of polyurethane-coated nylon, and they were filled by burning liquid propane gas. So successful was the combination that it sparked a remarkable revival of interest in hot-air ballooning. Today, there are regular hot-air balloon events all over the world, as well as many attempts to break long-distance records.

Light nylon-weave envelope

Envelope assembled by sewing together separate panels of material cut to a pattern

THE ENVELOPE
The balloon's envelope is made from a tough nylon material with a "ripstop" criss-cross weave to keep it from tearing. Normally, the crown of the balloon gets no hotter than 250°F (121°C), well below the melting point of nylon. But a temperature sensor is fitted at the top of the envelope, giving a continuous read-out in the basket, just in case.

UNCLE SAM
With the hot-air balloon revival, modern materials allowed balloon makers to break away from the traditional balloon shape. At first, they made simple shapes such as drink cans and bottles. Now you may see a complete French chateau or a two-humped camel floating gently through the sky.

Stainless-steel cables from the burner frame attached to strong nylon "load tapes" sewn on to the envelope

Cables end in quick-release spring clips for easy assembly and dismantling

Twin burners

Stainless-steel burner frame hangs from envelope and carries the cables that support the basket

BURNER SUPPORTS
Once the balloon is filled, the burners can hang from the balloon cables, but they are kept in position by a tube framework supported on four nylon rods. The gas supply pipes are strapped to the rods, inside a padded cover

Carrying handles for ground crew

INFLATION
Filling the balloon is perhaps the trickiest part of the entire balloon flight. Here the burner is being used to inflate the balloon on the ground.

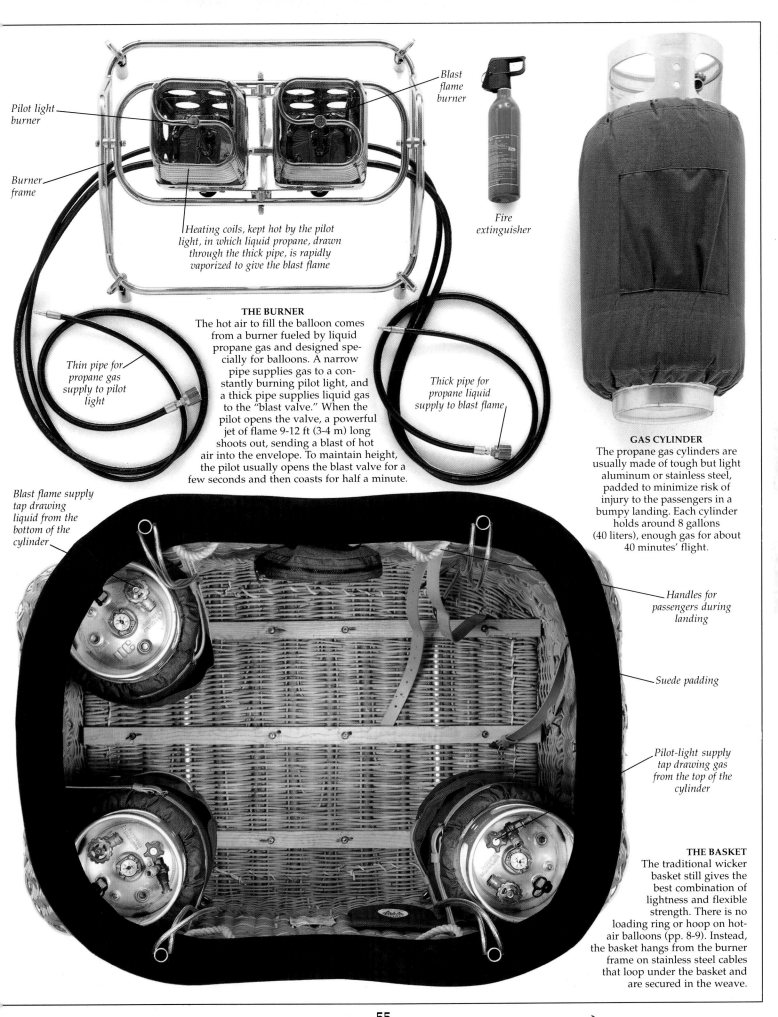

Pilot light burner

Burner frame

Blast flame burner

Fire extinguisher

Heating coils, kept hot by the pilot light, in which liquid propane, drawn through the thick pipe, is rapidly vaporized to give the blast flame

Thin pipe for propane gas supply to pilot light

THE BURNER

The hot air to fill the balloon comes from a burner fueled by liquid propane gas and designed specially for balloons. A narrow pipe supplies gas to a constantly burning pilot light, and a thick pipe supplies liquid gas to the "blast valve." When the pilot opens the valve, a powerful jet of flame 9-12 ft (3-4 m) long shoots out, sending a blast of hot air into the envelope. To maintain height, the pilot usually opens the blast valve for a few seconds and then coasts for half a minute.

Thick pipe for propane liquid supply to blast flame

GAS CYLINDER

The propane gas cylinders are usually made of tough but light aluminum or stainless steel, padded to minimize risk of injury to the passengers in a bumpy landing. Each cylinder holds around 8 gallons (40 liters), enough gas for about 40 minutes' flight.

Blast flame supply tap drawing liquid from the bottom of the cylinder

Handles for passengers during landing

Suede padding

Pilot-light supply tap drawing gas from the top of the cylinder

THE BASKET

The traditional wicker basket still gives the best combination of lightness and flexible strength. There is no loading ring or hoop on hot-air balloons (pp. 8-9). Instead, the basket hangs from the burner frame on stainless steel cables that loop under the basket and are secured in the weave.

Airship

It seemed the days of airships were over when they were involved in a number of tragic accidents just before World War II (p. 9), and the giants of the inter-war years did indeed vanish. Yet the airship's ability to stay aloft for hour after hour was useful for military tasks like submarine surveillance, and small, non-rigid airships filled with safe, nonflammable helium gas were still being made in the late 1960s. Then in the 1980s, Airship Industries began to produce a new generation of more substantial airships – made of modern materials, such as carbon-fiber and plastic composites, and filled with helium, not hydrogen like the early airships.

UP IN FLAMES
Airships filled with hydrogen gas were always in danger from fire. Almost half the 72 airships flown by the German forces in World War I went up in flames, and the inferno that destroyed the *Hindenburg* (p. 9) signaled the end for the giant airships.

Strengthened glass-fiber nose cone to take mooring cable

SKYSHIP 500HL
Although big – about 170 ft (50 m) long – the Skyship 500HL is a fraction of the size of the pre-war giant airships, such as the *Hindenburg,* which stretched 800 ft (245 m). However, there are plans to construct larger vessels, more than 400 ft (120 m) long. These will be able to stay in the air for a month or more at a time, to act as early warning stations for enemy attacks.

Automatic ballonet valve

Solid ballast for emergencies

Air scoops for filling ballonets

HANGING BASKET
Passengers and crew travel in a cabin beneath the envelope called the gondola. Molded from strong, lightweight carbon-fiber, it provides the same level of comfort as any modern aircraft. The flight deck, too, looks similar to that of a conventional plane – except there are no rudder pedals. In fact, since there are no ailerons (pp. 40-41), the pilot steers the airship by twisting the control column yoke to swing the rudder one way or the other.

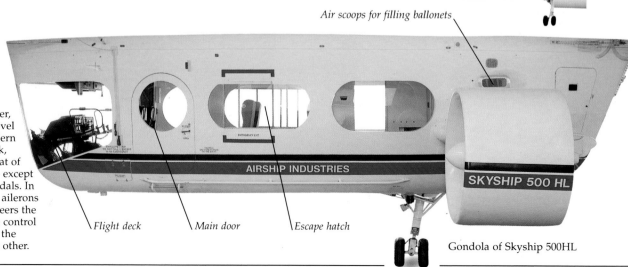

AIRSHIP INDUSTRIES

SKYSHIP 500 HL

Flight deck   *Main door*   *Escape hatch*

Gondola of Skyship 500HL

BLOWOUT
When the airship rises, eight valves like this open automatically to let air out of the airbags.

AIR BUBBLES
Inside the Skyship's helium-filled envelope are two air-filled bags called ballonets designed to reduce the loss of precious helium gas. As the airship climbs, atmospheric pressure drops and the gas expands. Rather than waste helium, automatic valves let out air from the ballonets instead (above). When the airship descends again, air is drawn in to refill the ballonets (right).

NOSE IN THE AIR
When climbing, the rear ballonet is kept fuller and heavier, helping the nose to come up. When descending, extra air is blown into the front ballonet, bringing the nose down.

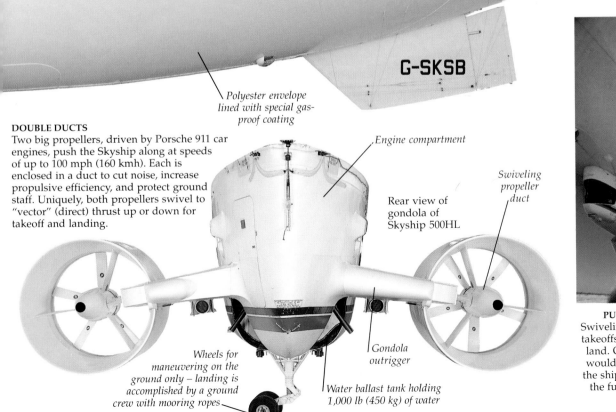

Rudder to steer the airship left or right

Elevator flaps to help climbing or diving

G-SKSB

Polyester envelope lined with special gas-proof coating

DOUBLE DUCTS
Two big propellers, driven by Porsche 911 car engines, push the Skyship along at speeds of up to 100 mph (160 kmh). Each is enclosed in a duct to cut noise, increase propulsive efficiency, and protect ground staff. Uniquely, both propellers swivel to "vector" (direct) thrust up or down for takeoff and landing.

Engine compartment

Rear view of gondola of Skyship 500HL

Swiveling propeller duct

Wheels for maneuvering on the ground only – landing is accomplished by a ground crew with mooring ropes

Gondola outrigger

Water ballast tank holding 1,000 lb (450 kg) of water

PUSHING UP AND DOWN
Swiveling propellers allow vertical takeoffs. They also help the ship to land. Otherwise precious helium would have to be let out to make the ship heavier – especially when the fuel tank is empty and light after a long flight.

A modern glider

ALTHOUGH GLIDERS played a prominent part in the pioneering days of aviation (pp. 10-11), interest in them waned after powered flight was achieved. The problem was that, without power, gliders can only fly, in effect, "downhill" and for a long time no glider could stay up for more than a few seconds. Then, in the early 1920s, it was found that gliders could ride up on the wind rising over a ridge or hill, so that skilled pilots could stay aloft for hours at a time. A few years later, it was discovered that even away from hills, glider pilots could get a lift from thermals – bubbles of rising air warmed by the ground. Ever since, the sport of gliding has become more and more popular, and the glider has now evolved into one of the most aerodynamically efficient and elegant of all flying machines.

MASTER GLIDER
Birds of prey showed how to glide upward on rising warm air.

LAUNCHING A GLIDER
Gliders can be launched in various ways. "Auto towing" means using a powerful car to pull the glider along on a long cable until it climbs into the air. "Winch launches" use a powerful winch in the same way. Both methods are cheap and quick, but will lift the glider no higher than 1,000 ft (300 m) or so. If the pilot cannot find lift from rising air quickly, the flight will last only a few minutes. An "air tow" – using a powered plane to tug the glider into the air (below and right) – is much more effective, but time-consuming and expensive.

Tug makes normal takeoff with glider in tow

Powered "tug" plane tows glider on a 130 ft (40 m) tow rope

Air brakes emerge from the wings at right-angles to steepen the descent for landing

SLIPPERY SAILPLANE
Modern gliders such as this Schleicher K23 single-seater are made from GRP (glass reinforced plastic). GRP is not only strong and light, but can also be molded to give a super-smooth, low-drag surface. With such smooth lines and carefully profiled wings, a glider like this is very efficient aerodynamically – with, typically, a "glide ratio" of better than 1:45. This means it will usually drop only 1 ft (0.3 m) for every 45 ft (15 m) it flies. Competition gliders perform even better.

Down-turned wingtips stop ailerons hitting the ground when landing and also reduce air turbulence at the wingtip

Aileron

Instrument panel

SLING SHOT
In the days when many gliding clubs were on hilltops, a "bungee" launch was often enough. A team ran toward edge of the hill pulling the glider on an elastic rope. As the glider came "unstuck" from the ground, it catapulted into the air.

Tow rope attached here for winch launch or auto tow

Elevator

T tail

Glider releases tow rope at desired height

Freed from the glider, the tug accelerates rapidly and dives away

SILENT WINGS
Large gliders like the Airspeed Horsa (left) were sometimes used during World War II for landing troops and equipment silently behind enemy lines. Once spotted, however, they were slow and very vulnerable.

SLIM TUBE
The slim, tapering fuselage is carefully shaped to minimize drag. Even around the cockpit, it is as narrow as possible, and near the tail it shrinks to a diameter of less than 1 ft (under 30 cm). The tail fin itself is usually T-shaped, not only for aerodynamic performance, but also to protect the tailplanes from damage by tall crops if the glider has to make a forced landing in a field.

Wing tanks holding water ballast which adds weight for extra speed on long straight flights – and may be jettisoned later for circling slowly

Semireclining pilot's seat to keep cockpit low

WINGSPAN
All wings lose some of their lifting power at the tips because air flowing underneath curls over the top. The longer the wing is, the less lift is lost, so gliders have very long wings.

EVW

Rudder

Tow rope attached here for air tow

Kites for people

THE IDEA OF FLYING with a pair of wings alone seems to have been forgotten after the deaths of Lilienthal and other pioneer gliders around 1900 (pp.10-11). Then in the 1940s, an American named Francis Rogallo created a new kite plane using a fabric delta (triangular) wing. It was developed first simply as a steerable parachute for bringing equipment back to Earth from space. But some people began to fly Rogallo wings by hanging beneath the wing and steering by shifting their weight. The idea caught on. Soon "hang gliders" were running off hills all over the world. Hang gliding is now one of the most popular aerial sports.

SPREADING WINGS
The earliest Rogallo-type hang gliders dropped quickly, achieving a glide ratio (p. 58) of only 1:2.5. So flights were exciting but short. Wings have gradually been improved, however, and are now long and narrow – much more like conventional wings than the original delta. The frame is also covered with fabric both on top and underneath to give a more efficient aerofoil section. The result is that glide ratios are now 1:14 or better, and hang gliders are able, like gliders, to take advantage of thermals to make flights of over 100 miles (160 km).

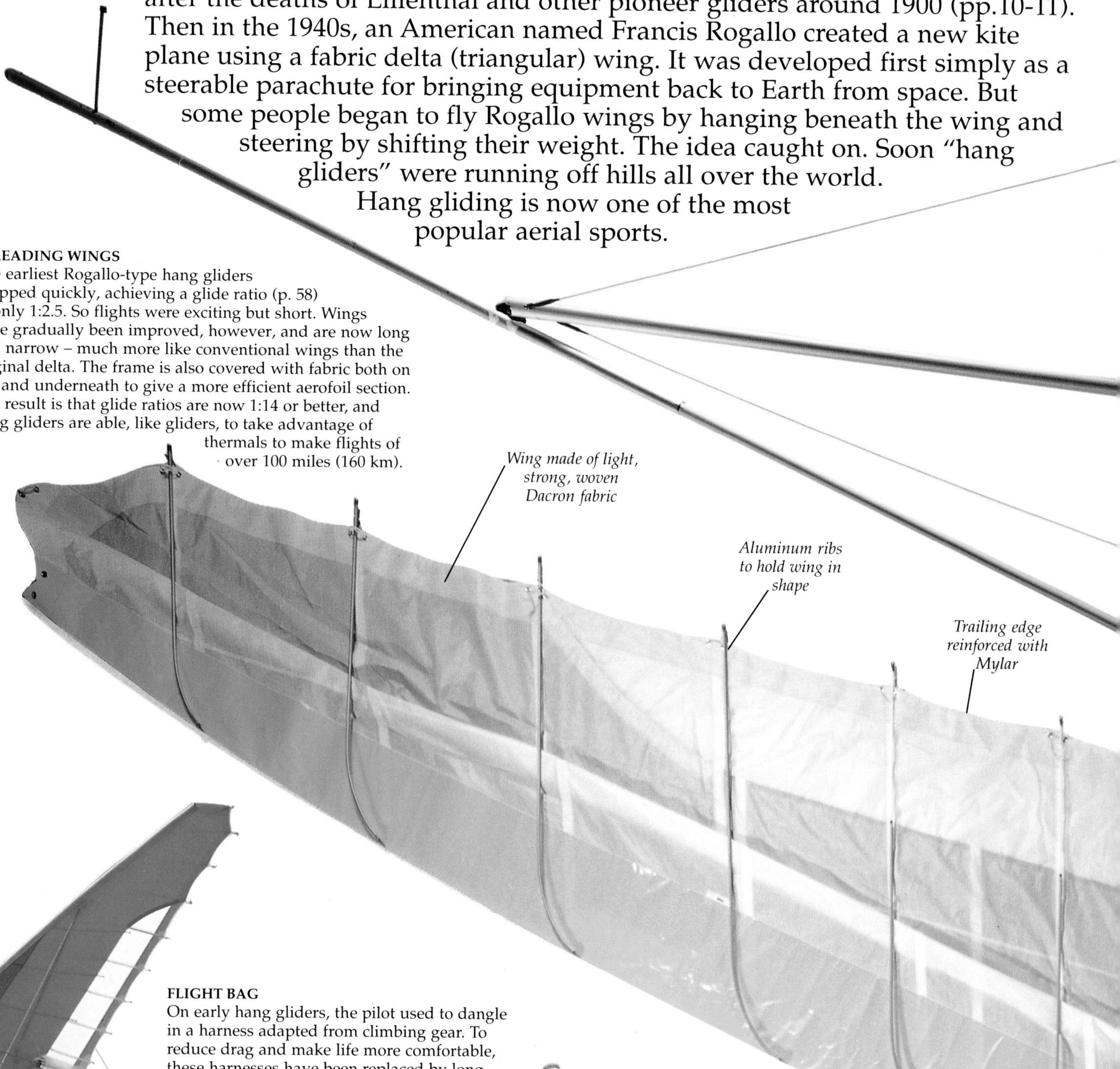

Wing made of light, strong, woven Dacron fabric

Aluminum ribs to hold wing in shape

Trailing edge reinforced with Mylar

FLIGHT BAG
On early hang gliders, the pilot used to dangle in a harness adapted from climbing gear. To reduce drag and make life more comfortable, these harnesses have been replaced by long "body bags." Body bags are so supportive and snug that a pilot can make flights of several hours without getting tired or cold.

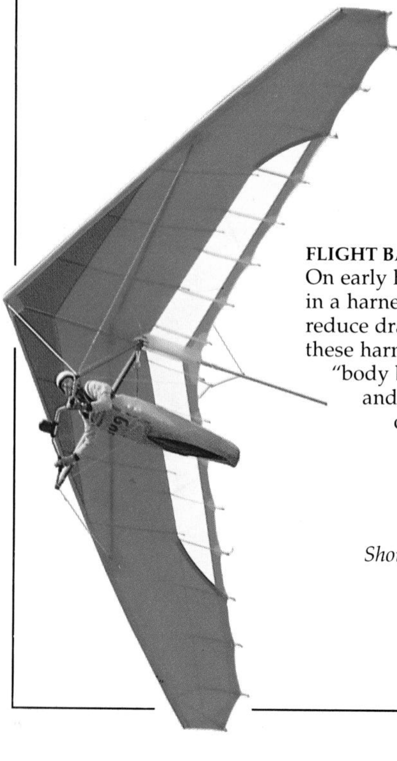

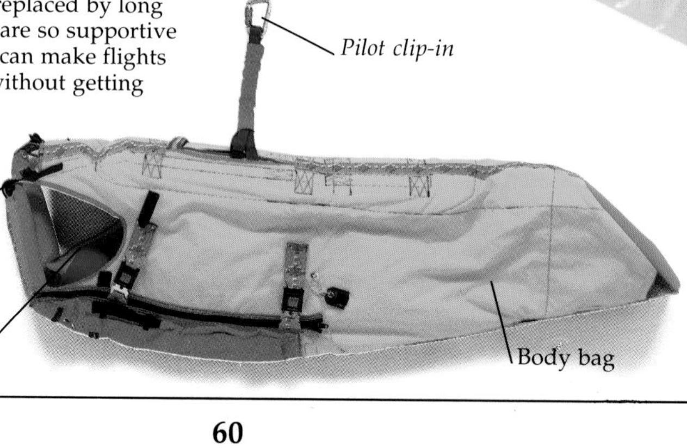

Pilot clip-in

Shoulder strap

Armhole

Body bag

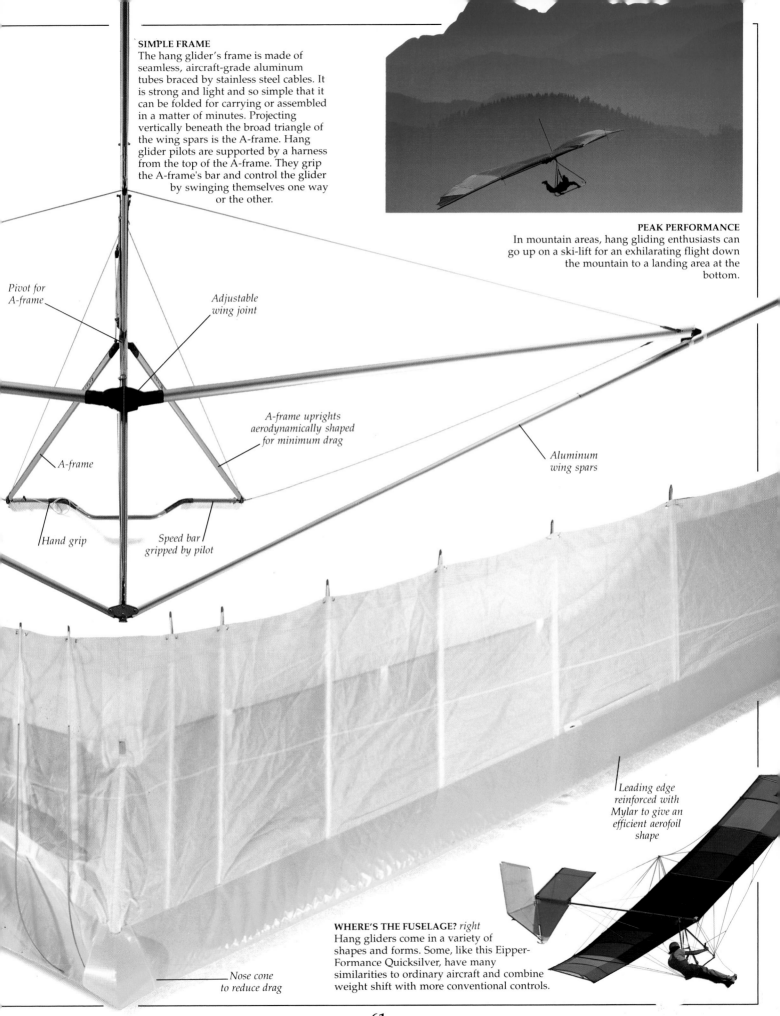

SIMPLE FRAME
The hang glider's frame is made of seamless, aircraft-grade aluminum tubes braced by stainless steel cables. It is strong and light and so simple that it can be folded for carrying or assembled in a matter of minutes. Projecting vertically beneath the broad triangle of the wing spars is the A-frame. Hang glider pilots are supported by a harness from the top of the A-frame. They grip the A-frame's bar and control the glider by swinging themselves one way or the other.

PEAK PERFORMANCE
In mountain areas, hang gliding enthusiasts can go up on a ski-lift for an exhilarating flight down the mountain to a landing area at the bottom.

*Pivot for
A-frame*

*Adjustable
wing joint*

*A-frame uprights
aerodynamically shaped
for minimum drag*

*Aluminum
wing spars*

A-frame

Hand grip

*Speed bar
gripped by pilot*

*Leading edge
reinforced with
Mylar to give an
efficient aerofoil
shape*

*Nose cone
to reduce drag*

WHERE'S THE FUSELAGE? *right*
Hang gliders come in a variety of shapes and forms. Some, like this Eipper-Formance Quicksilver, have many similarities to ordinary aircraft and combine weight shift with more conventional controls.

Portable planes

From the first days of powered flying, enthusiasts dreamed of a small aircraft cheap enough and practical enough to be flown by ordinary people. Yet until recently, even planes like the basic and popular De Havilland Moth (p. 43) remained expensive, complicated machines. Then in 1973, Australian hang glider pioneer Bill Bennett began experimenting with a hang glider and a chainsaw motor driving a pusher propeller behind the pilot. It was not altogether safe, but it worked, and the "microlight" was born. Since then, the way the engine is fitted has become much more practical and safe, and the frame has been improved to take the extra load. Microlights are now flown all over the world. Some retain flexible wings (flexwing) like hang gliders. Others, especially in the U.S. and Australia (where they are known as "ultralights"), have developed into miniature aircraft with fixed wings and control surfaces.

Aluminum wing spar

Tensioning cable

THE FIRST MICROLIGHT?
Brazilian pioneer Alberto Santos-Dumont's tiny No. 19 monoplane had a wingspan of just 18 ft (6 m) and was perhaps the first microlight. He designed it in Paris in 1907 as an aerial "runabout" and could unrig it to carry it on his car.

WIDE WING
Like the hang glider on pages 60-61, a flexwing microlight like this Solar Wings Pegasus Q has a shallow triangular wing of Dacron. But it is made broader than the hang glider to lift the extra weight of the engine, trike, and two crew members.

Laminated wooden propeller, mounted safely out of the way behind the crew, to push the aircraft along

Air intake and filter

50 hp water-cooled, twin-cylinder Rotax engine

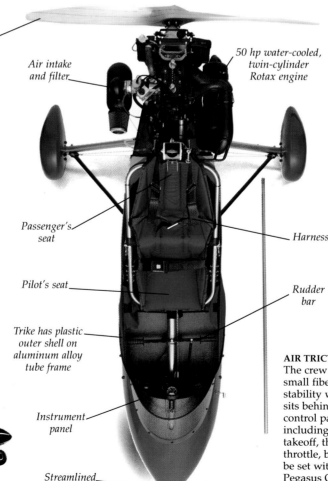

PEGASUS IN FLIGHT
Flexwing microlights like this are extremely safe and predictable, and will not stall until the speed drops below 24 mph (40 kmh).

Passenger's seat

Harness

Pilot's seat

Rudder bar

Trike has plastic outer shell on aluminum alloy tube frame

Instrument panel

Streamlined nose cone

AIR TRICYCLE
The crew of a flexwing microlight usually sits inside a small fiberglass car or "trike," with three-wheels for stability when landing and taking off. The passenger sits behind and slightly above the pilot, who faces a control panel with a small range of instruments including airspeed indicator and altimeter. For takeoff, the pilot revs up the engine with the foot throttle, but during flight, a steady cruise speed can be set with the hand throttle. The Solar Wings Pegasus Q can climb at over 900 ft (270 m) a minute and cruises at 90 mph (144 kmh).

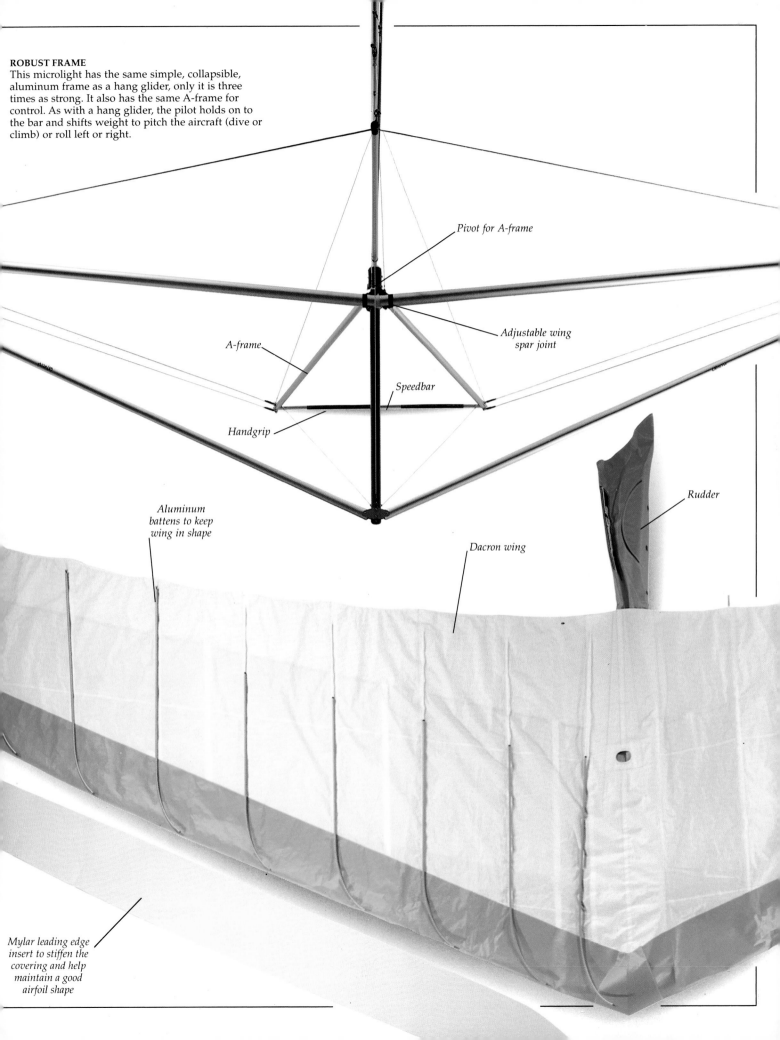

ROBUST FRAME
This microlight has the same simple, collapsible, aluminum frame as a hang glider, only it is three times as strong. It also has the same A-frame for control. As with a hang glider, the pilot holds on to the bar and shifts weight to pitch the aircraft (dive or climb) or roll left or right.

Pivot for A-frame

Adjustable wing spar joint

A-frame

Speedbar

Handgrip

Aluminum battens to keep wing in shape

Rudder

Dacron wing

Mylar leading edge insert to stiffen the covering and help maintain a good airfoil shape

Did you know?

AMAZING FACTS

Wright brothers' first flight

The first "passengers" in a free flight were a sheep, a duck, and a rooster, which in 1783 flew in a wicker basket suspended from a balloon designed by the Montgolfier brothers.

The first aerial stowaway was a young man called Fontaine, who jumped into a Montgolfier hot-air balloon just as it was taking off in January 1784.

The *Flyer* made four flights on December 17, 1903, with the Wright brothers taking it in turn to fly. The longest flight of the day (59 seconds) was made by Wilbur, at 853 ft (260 m).

The first woman to make a solo flight was Baroness Raymonde de Laroche, in 1909. A year later, she became the first woman to receive a pilot's license, issued by the Aéro Club of France.

The first solo flight across the Atlantic was made by Charles Lindbergh in 1927, in a Ryan monoplane called the *Spirit of St. Louis*.

One of Lindbergh's challenges on his 33.5 hour flight across the Atlantic was to stay awake. He did this by pinching himself and opening the aircraft's side window to get a blast of fresh air.

The first helicopter flight was made by French mechanic Paul Cornu in 1907 when his machine lifted and hovered for 20 seconds.

The Blue Max (the nickname of the highest German honor for service during World War I, the *Ordre pour le Merité*) was named after Max Immelmann, a flying "ace" and award-winner.

In the early days of flying, one of the most famous awards was the Schneider Trophy. The first Schneider seaplane air race, held in Monaco in 1913, was won by Maurice Prevost, the only pilot to complete the course, traveling at an average speed of 45.7 mph (73.6 kmh).

The first all-woman air race took place in the United States in 1929 and became known as the "Powder-puff Derby." Amelia Earhart (see p. 67) took part.

The first modern commercial airplane was the Boeing 247, built in 1933. It carried just 10 passengers.

Schneider Trophy poster

The Boeing 747–400ER can fly around 8,800 miles (14,200 km) without stopping to refuel.

The longest man-powered flight was made by Greek cycle champion Kanellos Kanellopoulos in April 1988 in the *Daedalus*, by pedaling almost 75 miles (120 km) in four hours.

In 1999, the *Breitling Orbiter 3* became the first balloon to fly non-stop around the world. Then, in 2002, Steve Fossett did it solo. His flight took 13 days.

Charles Lindbergh

Steve Fossett

QUESTIONS AND ANSWERS

Q Who was the first person to fly?

A The first person to fly in free flight was Jean François Pilâtre de Rosier, who, accompanied by the Marquis d'Arlandes, flew for 23 minutes and travelled 5.5 miles (9 km) in a Montgolfier balloon on November 21, 1783. However, the world's first aviator is considered to be Otto Lilienthal, who invented a practical hang-glider and became the first person to make repeated controlled flights in the early 1890s. Orville Wright made the world's first powered airplane flight on December 17, 1903 in Kitty Hawk, North Carolina, in *Flyer*. The flight lasted 12 seconds, and the aircraft traveled 120 ft (37 m).

Airbus A3XX (now called the A380)

Q How did the first aviators know where they were going?

A The first airplanes had no instruments, so to find out where they were, aviators simply looked out of the plane for landmarks, such as a church tower. To find out their height, they had small pocket altimeters similar to those used by mountaineers.

Q Why are aircraft propellers twisted?

A Aircraft propellers rotate faster at the tips than near the center. If the blade was the same angle at the tip as the center, the air resistance on the tip would be too great, slowing down the propeller or bending the blade. Twisting the blade ensures the air resistance is the same over the propeller's whole surface.

Twisted propeller

LVG CVI 1917

Q What is the world's largest commercial airplane?

A The largest commercial airliner is currently the wide-bodied Boeing 747-400, which is 232 ft (70 m) long with a wingspan of 211 ft (64 m) and can carry around 420 passengers. However, when it goes into production, the largest commercial airliner will be the Airbus A380, built by Airbus Industries. The A380 will have a wingspan of almost 262 ft (80 m) and will be able to carry 555 passengers in three different classes of seating.

Q Why do most jet airliners use turbofan jet engines rather than turbojets?

A Although turbofan jet airliners such as Boeing can only travel half the speed of turbojet-powered Concorde, turbofans are quieter and cheaper to operate. Concorde was banned from some airports because of its supersonic boom as it crosses the sound barrier.

Q Will airliners be able to fly faster than Concorde?

A Several countries, including the United States through NASA's Hyper-X program, are currently developing aircraft that will be able to fly at hypersonic speeds—that is, five times faster than the speed of sound.

Record Breakers

LARGEST AIRPLANE
The Hughes H-4 Hercules flying boat, the *Spruce Goose*, was the world's largest airplane, with a wingspan measuring 320 ft (97.5 m).

SMALLEST AIRPLANE
The smallest biplane is *Bumble Bee Two*, which is just 8.7 ft (2.64 m) long and weighs 400 lb (180 kg).

HEAVIEST AIRPLANE
The Antonov An-225 *Mriya* (meaning "Dream") is the heaviest aircraft ever to fly, weighing a staggering 590 tons (600 tonnes). The plane has six engines, and its cargo hold is 142 ft (43 m) long.

FASTEST COMMERCIAL AIRLINER
Concorde flew at a maximum cruising speed of Mach 2.05, or 1,354 mph (2,179 kmh), which is twice the speed of sound. Although it traveled more than twice as fast as the Boeing 747), it seated just 128 passengers.

BUSIEST AIRPORT
O'Hare International Airport in Chicago was the world's busiest airport in 2001, in terms of take-offs and landings. Hartsfield International Airport in Atlanta, Georgia, was the busiest in terms of passenger numbers, with 80.1 million the same year.

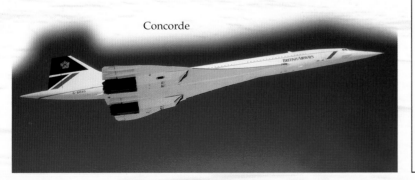
Concorde

Chicago O'Hare airport

Who's who?

THE HUGE ADVANCES IN AVIATION made in the last 100 years were only possible because of the bravery and dedication of the pioneers of early flying machines. Here are some of those pioneers, and a few of the many people involved in the production of great aircraft, from designers and engineers to manufacturers and test pilots.

PIONEERS OF FLIGHT

JOSEPH AND ETIENNE MONTGOLFIER
French inventors Joseph (1740–1810) and Etienne (1745–99) were sons of a paper manufacturer from southeast France. Interested in how paper was lifted up a chimney when put on a fire, they created the first hot-air balloon in 1782.

SIR GEORGE CAYLEY (1773–1857)
English engineer and pioneer of aviation who developed the basic principles of heavier-than-air flight, being (among other things) the first inventor to work out how a wing works, realizing the advantages of a cambered surface. In 1853, he built the first successful man-carrying glider.

HENRI GIFFARD (1825–82)
French engineer and inventor who, in 1852, built a cigar-shaped balloon fitted with a light steam engine, propeller, and rudder and succeeded in steering it a distance of 17 miles (27 km)—the forerunner of the modern dirigible, or airship

Otto Lilienthal

FERDINAND VON ZEPPELIN (1838–1917)
German army officer who constructed a dirigible or rigid airship (named a zeppelin) between 1897 and 1900, which first flew on July 2, 1900. Zeppelin later set up a company to build a fleet of airships.

CLÉMENT ADER (1841–1925)
French engineer who built a steam-powered, bat-winged plane called *Éole* between 1882 and 1890. He made the first piloted powered take-off in it in October 1890, covering a distance of 165 ft (50 m)

OTTO LILIENTHAL (1848–96)
German aeronautical inventor and pioneer of gliders who studied the flight of birds in order to build a heavier-than-air flying machine, publishing a book based on his research called *Bird Flight as the Basis of Aviation* (1889). He then built a series of fixed-wing monoplane and biplane gliders, making over 1,000 flights. He was killed in a flying accident near Berlin when the wind threw his glider out of control.

Wilbur Wright

ORVILLE AND WILBUR WRIGHT
Orville (1871–1948) and Wilbur (1867–1912) were self-taught American airplane pioneers and the first to fly in a heavier-than-air powered aircraft at Kitty Hawk, North Carolina, on December 17, 1903. They patented their flying machine and, in 1909, formed an aircraft production company.

LOUIS BLERIOT (1872–1936)
French airman who pioneered the monoplane aircraft with a single wing, separate tail, and front engine. On July 25, 1909, he made the first flight across the English Channel in his small Type XI aircraft, becoming an instant celebrity.

INVENTORS, ENGINEERS, AND DESIGNERS

ELMER AMBROSE SPERRY (1860–1930)
American inventor of many new devices including the gyroscopic compass (1911) and gyroscope-stabilized instruments for airplanes, such as the directional gyro, the gyro horizon, and the drift indicator. His son, Lawrence Sperry (1892–1923) designed a retractable undercarriage.

SIDNEY CAMM (1893–1966)
English aircraft designer who became chief designer of the Hawker Engineering Company (later Hawker Siddeley Aviation). Planes he designed included the Fury, Hart, and Demon biplanes; the jet-engined Sea Hawk; and the Harrier Jump-Jet.

Igor Ivanovich Sikorsky

JUAN DE LA CIERVA (1895–1936)
Spanish inventor who developed the "autogiro"—a rotor craft with a freely rotating wing—that aimed to be a safe form of air transport.

FRANK WHITTLE (1907–96)
British pioneer of jet aircraft who trained as a pilot in the RAF (Royal Air Force), becoming a test pilot. He devised a jet-propelling, gas-turbine engine, later used in a Gloster aircraft in 1941. His invention led to the worldwide use of jet engines in high-speed, high-flying aircraft.

IGOR IVANOVICH SIKORSKY (1889–1972)
Russian-born aeronautical engineer who built airplanes, flying boats, then, in 1939, the first successful helicopter, the VS-300.

MANUFACTURERS

William Edward Boeing

HUGO JUNKERS (1859–1935)
German aircraft engineer whose company built the first successful all-metal airplane in 1915, then, in 1916, the first light-alloy airplane.

WILLIAM EDWARD BOEING (1881–1956)
American aircraft manufacturer who formed the Pacific Aero-Products Co. in 1916. The company was renamed the Boeing Airplane Company in 1917, becoming the largest manufacturer of aircraft in the world.

ANTHONY FOKKER (1890–1939)
Dutch aircraft engineer who built his first plane in 1911, and founded the Fokker aircraft factory in Germany in 1913, which made aircraft for the German air force during World War I. He immigrated to the United States in 1922, becoming president of the Fokker Aircraft Corporation of America.

GEOFFREY DE HAVILLAND (1882–1965)
British aircraft designer and test pilot at the Royal Aircraft Factory at Farnborough, England. He started his own company in 1920, which built the DH-60 Moth light airplane, the Mosquito, and the Comet, the world's first jetliner.

DONALD WILLS DOUGLAS (1892–1981)
American aircraft designer and manufacturer who set up a company (David-Douglas Co.) in 1920. Its successful aircraft include the Douglas World Cruisers (two of which made an historic around-the-world flight in 1924) and the jet-engineed DC-3, DC-8, DC-9, and DC-10. The company merged with McDonnell in 1967.

ERNST HEINRICH HEINKEL (1888–1958)
German aircraft engineer and manufacturer who set up his own company in 1922, making a series of seaplanes, flying boats, and military aircraft. He also built the first jet plane (the HE-178) in 1939 and the first rocket-powered aircraft (the HE-176).

ALLAN HAINES LOCKHEED (1889–1969)
American aircraft manufacturer who started the Alco Hydro-Aeroplane Co. in 1913, then, in 1916, Loughhead Aircraft, which was relaunched as Lockheed Aircraft Co. in 1926.

Donald Wills Douglas

AVIATORS

Amelia Earhart

JOHN WILLIAM ALCOCK (1892–1919)
English aviator and, in June 1919, with Arthur Whitten Brown as navigator, the first person to fly across the Atlantic non-stop, from Newfoundland to Ireland. Shortly afterwards, Alcock was killed in an airplane accident in France.

ARTHUR WHITTEN BROWN (1886–1948)
British aviator and navigator with John William Alock on the first non-stop crossing of the Atlantic.

MAX IMMELMANN (1890–1916)
Flying "ace" of World War I; had a maneuver (the Immelmann turn) named after him, comprising of a half-loop followed by a half-roll, said to be a way for pilots to escape pursuit or mount an attack. He was killed in action in 1916.

CHARLES KINGSFORD SMITH (1897–1935)
Australian pilot who made the first flight across the Pacific from the United States to Australia in 1928, and also the first non-stop flight across Australia, and the first flight from Australia to New Zealand. He formed Australian National Airways in 1928. He and his crew later disappeared over the Bay of Bengal.

WILEY POST (1899–1935)
American aviator who set a record time for flying around the world in the Lockheed Vega *Winnie Mae*, in June 1931, with navigator Harold Gatty. The trip took 8 days, 15 hours, and 51 minutes. In 1933, Post became the first person to fly around the world solo. He was killed in an air crash in 1935.

AMELIA EARHART (1897–1937)
American aviator and the first woman to fly the Atlantic, from Newfoundland to Wales, on June 17, 1928, in a Lockheed Vega. Earhart and her navigator, Fred Noonan, disappeared over the Pacific in July 1937, during an attempt to fly around the world.

CHARLES AUGUSTUS LINDBERGH (1902–74)
American aviator who worked as an airmail pilot and became famous after he made the first solo non-stop flight across the Atlantic, from New York to Paris, in May 1927, in his plane the *Spirit of St Louis*.

AMY JOHNSON (1903–1941)
British aviator who got her pilot's license in 1928, then, just two years later, made a solo flight from England to Australia in 19 and a half days, in a de Havilland DH-60 Moth nicknamed "Jason."

CHARLES "CHUCK" YEAGER (1923–)
American test pilot who fought with the U.S. Army Air Corps during World War II. Yeager became the first person to fly faster than the speed of sound, at around 700 mph (1,100 kmh), or Mach 1.06, on October 14, 1947, in a Bell XS-1 rocket plane. The plane was nicknamed "Glennis" after Yeager's wife.

Charles "Chuck" Yeager

Find out more

YOU CAN FIND OUT a lot about the history of air travel by visiting museums, where you can see some of the famous early planes of the pioneers, or even have try out a flight simulator. There are also air shows and ballooning events around the world where it is possible to see all kinds of civilian and military aircraft, hot-air balloons, and airships up close. The Internet is a great resource for finding out about events near you or around the world.

TAKE A RIDE
At some museums and air shows, it is possible to take a ride in an airplane. For example, visitors to the Old Rhinebeck Aerodrome in Rhinebeck, New York, can take a ride in an open-cockpit biplane (pictured above). You can also take a flight in a vintage Tiger Moth or de Havilland Dragon Rapide at the Imperial War Museum at Duxford, England.

The Boeing Sonic Cruiser will fly at Mach 0.95 or more.

Jonathan Wolfe's Fiesta F50 balloon, the Gloria Caeli, at Châtellerault, France

BALLOON FESTIVALS
The Montgolfier world ballooning championships are held every two years, offering plenty of events such as races, dramatic night flights, and a chance to see the latest models of competitive or fiesta balloons. The 15th festival was held at Châtellerault in France in 2002, and the 2004 festival was held in Australia.

IN THE PRESS
New developments in aircraft design and manufacture are often reported in newspapers. You can also see the latest models of aircraft at air shows, such as this Boeing Sonic Cruiser, which was unveiled at the Paris Airshow, held at Le Bourget Airport in 2001.

AIR SHOWS
Many countries hold air shows at which you can see hundreds of exhibits from all over the world. The Paris Airshow began in 1908 and is held each summer at Le Bourget Airport in Paris, France. Farnborough International, an air show organized by the Society of British Aerospace Companies, is held outside of London, England. In 2002, it had over 1,000 exhibits from 32 countries. The London Airshow and Balloon Festival is held every June at London International Airport in Ontario, Canada. As well as getting up close to a range of aircraft, visitors can watch flying demonstrations and take balloon and helicopter rides.

AERIAL DISPLAYS

At many airshows and other events, you can see daring aeronautical displays. One of the most famous aeronautical teams is England's Royal Air Forces' Red Arrows. You can log on to their Web site (www.raf.mod.uk/reds) to check out some of their amazing maneuvers on screen.

Red Arrow aeronautical display team

One of the Red Arrows' 12 Hawk jet trainer aircraft

Cockpit with realistic data-display instruments

HANDS-ON

Some museums, such the RAF Museum in London, England, and the Cité des Sciences, a science museum in Paris, France, have hands-on displays where you can operate an aircraft flight simulator with feed-in and feed-back computer data. Some computer game companies also produce flight simulation games so you can test your flying and landing skills in all sorts of weather conditions.

PLANE-SPOTTING

Some airports have viewing terraces or galleries where you can watch aircraft land, re-fuel, and take off. At some busy airports, as many as 50 aircraft take off and land every hour. Some are huge international airliners en route to other continents. Others are smaller planes making domestic flights. Some people go especially to see particular types of aircraft, looking out for the distinctive insignia and colors of various national airlines.

Museums to visit

SMITHSONIAN INSTITUTION NATIONAL AIR AND SPACE MUSEUM, WASHINGTON, D.C.
www.nasm.si.edu/
This huge museum has over 350 aircraft in its collection, many of which are on display. Worth seeing are the historic Wright 1903 *Flyer,* the Ryan *Spirit of St. Louis,* and the Bell X-1.

THE NEW ENGLAND AIR MUSEUM, WINDSOR LOCKS, CT
www.neam.org
This aviation museum holds many fascinating exhibits from aircraft and engine displays to the Tuskegee Airmen, Early French Aviation, and a History of Air Mail.

ROYAL AIR FORCE MUSEUM, HENDON, LONDON, UK
www.rafmuseum.org.uk/
This museum has over 200 aircraft in its collection, many on permanent display. Highlights include:
• the Milestones of Flight gallery, which traces the history of aviation and includes such historic aircraft as the Blériot XI
• getting hands-on in the Fun 'n' Flight gallery

THE INTREPID SEA, AIR, AND SPACE MUSEUM, NEW YORK, NY
www.intrepidmuseum.org
The scale of this old aircraft carrier gives the Intrepid museum an impressive backdrop to its aircraft collection. On its 900-foot-long flight deck are the majority of the museum's aircraft collection, including the jA-6 Intruder and the FJ-3 Fury, which once actually flew off the Intrepid as part of her air group.

SAN DIEGO AEROSPACE MUSEUM, SAN DIEGO, CA
www.aerospacemuseum.org/links.html
Air travel unfolds at the large San Diego Aerospace Museum with a model of the Montgolfier brothers' hot air balloon of 1783 and follows with exhibits charting the dawn of powered flight, air combat in World War I, and beyond. Highlights include:
• a Spitfire Mk OVI
• a A-4 Skyhawk jet
• a Navy F6F Hellcat

EEA AIRVENTURE MUSEUM, OSHKOSH, WI
http://museum.eaa.org/
Oshkosh, Wisconsin, hosts the largest air show in the US and the EEA AirVenture Museum. This large museum houses a collection of more than 250 historic airplanes and boasts five movie theaters. The "hands-on" Hanger X is an exciting interactive gallery for kids of all ages. Also not to be missed is the Eagle Hanger, which displays a tribute to World War II aviation.

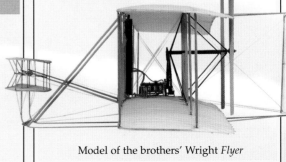

Model of the brothers' Wright Flyer

Glossary

Airship

AERODYNAMICS The study of the movement of objects through air

AIRFOIL Curved wing shape in which the upper surface is longer (from leading to trailing edge) than its lower surface

AILERON Flap on an airplane's trailing edge enabling an airplane to tilt to one side (called rolling or banking)

AIRBRAKE Surface that can be extended from an aircraft's wings to slow it down or steepen its descent

AIRSHIP Long, thin, lighter-than-air craft usually filled with helium or hot air; often steered by swiveling propellers to help with take off and landing

ALTIMETER Instrument used to measure an airplane's altitude, or height

ARTIFICIAL HORIZON Instrument used to indicate an aircraft's position in relation to the horizon, enabling a pilot to land more safely in poor weather or at night; often called a gyro-horizon

AUTOGIRO Craft with a conventional propeller and a rotor, which is spun by the action of air flowing through its disc from below; forerunner of the helicopter

AUTOMATIC PILOT (or autopilot) Electronic system that automatically stabilizes an aircraft and can put it back on its original flightpath after a disturbance, such as turbulence. In modern aircraft, the autopilot can be set so that the aircraft follows a certain course.

BALLONET Air-filled compartment inside an airship's envelope (which contains lighter-than-air helium gas), used to control the airship's height. Letting air out makes the airship lighter and rise; pumping air in makes the airship heavier and sink.

BIPLANE Fixed-wing aircraft with two wings

BOGIE Type of landing leg on an aircraft with two or more pairs of wheels

CAMBER Curve on the wing section of an airplane

COCKPIT Compartment in an airplane's fuselage for the pilot(s) and, sometimes, other crew

CRT Cathode-ray tube screen displaying flight and navigation information in a aircraft's "glass cockpit." CRTs have now been replaced by liquid crystal screens in most modern aircraft.

DIRIGIBLE Able to be steered

DOPE Airplane varnish painted onto fabric to make it stronger and tighter

DRAG Pressure of air slowing down an airplane when in flight

DRIFT INDICATOR Instrument that shows an airplane's angle of drift (its sideways movement because of crosswind)

Helicopter

ELEVATOR Flap on an airplane's tail that enables the airplane to move up or down (called pitching)

ELEVONS Wing control surfaces with the same functions as ailerons and elevators

ENVELOPE Casing (usually coated in nylon) of an airship that contains the gas used to provide lift

FLYING BOAT Airplane with a watertight hull, allowing it to move on water

FUSELAGE Body of an aircraft; from the French word "fuseler" meaning to shape like a spindle

"GLASS COCKPIT" Cockpit in which traditional instruments are replaced by electronic displays on color cathode-ray tube (CRT) or liquid crystal screens

GLIDER Unpowered aircraft with a wide wingspan that uses currents of hot, rising air (thermals) to stay airborne; controlled with a rudder, elevators, and ailerons

GONDALA Airship's cabin in which the passengers and crew travel

HANG-GLIDER Unpowered craft that uses thermals for lift, made of material stretched across a simple frame forming a wing. The pilot hangs below the wing in a harness or body-bag and steers by shifting his or her weight from side to side

HELICOPTER Aircraft powered, lifted, and steered by rotating blades and which can take off vertically, fly slowly, hover, and move in any direction. Often used for traffic surveillance and rescue work because of its maneuverability.

HOT-AIR BALLOON Lighter-than-air craft used mainly for recreation. Modern hot-air balloons use propane burners carried above the balloon's basket to heat up the air inside the envelope. (*see also* ENVELOPE)

Flying boat

JOYSTICK Control column used to "steer" an aircraft so it can dive, climb, or roll

LEADING EDGE The front edge of (for example) a wing, rotor, or tail

LIFT Upward force created by the way in which air flows around an aircraft wing (*see also* AIRFOIL)

LONGERON Part of an aircraft's structure that runs the length of the fuselage

MACH NUMBER Ratio of an airplane's air speed to the speed of sound in the given conditions (such as height, air density, and temperature); named after the Austrian physicist Ernst Mach (1838–1916). Mach 1 is the speed of sound, or about 659 mph (1,060 kmh) at 36,000 ft (11,000 m); Mach 2 is twice the speed of sound, and so on.

MICROLIGHT Powered hang-glider with a small engine and open fiberglass car, called a trike; also called an "ultralight"

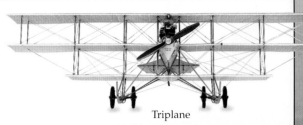
Triplane

Ultralight

MONOCOQUE Fuselage with no internal bracing in which nearly all the structural load is carried by the skin

MONOPLANE Fixed wing aircraft with a single wing

NON-RIGID Type of airship with no internal framework, in which shape is maintained by the pressure of gas and air ballonets inside

ORNITHOPTER Aircraft propelled by flapping wings

PITCH Rotating or tilting of a aircraft nose-up and nose-down by raising or lowering the elevators on the tailplane (*see also* ELEVATOR, TAILPLANE)

PROPELLER Rotating blades that drive an aircraft forward

RIGID Airship with an internal framework

ROLL Movement of an aircraft so one wing tip rises and the other falls by adjusting the ailerons

RUDDER Vertical, flat surface for steering an airplane to the right or left

SCARFF RING Mounting for hand-operated machine guns, allowing gunners to swivel the gun and fire in many directions.

SPAR Structural support in a wing running the length of the wing

SPEED OF SOUND The speed of sound is around 761 mph (1,225 kmh) at sea level and falls the higher you go into the sky. Above around 3,280 ft (1,000 m) the speed of sound stays the same, at around 659 mph (1,060 kmh).

STALL When aircraft's lift is lost, causing the plane to pitch downward, possibly going into a spin

STRUT Vertical support or brace that resists pressure; for example, between the longerons in a fuselage (*see also* FUSELAGE, LONGERON)

SUPERCHARGER Device that forces extra air into an airplane's engine to increase power at high altitudes

SUPERSONIC Faster than the speed of sound

TAILPLANE Wings at the back of an aircraft to provide stability when pitching and to which the elevators are often attached (*see also* PITCH)

TILT-ROTOR Aircraft with rotors enabling it to take off vertically, swivel, then be powered forward

TRAILING EDGE The rear edge of (for example) a wing, rotor, or tail

TRIPLANE Fixed wing aircraft with three wings, such as the German Fokker Triplane of the early 1900s

TURBOFAN Type of gas-turbine engine in which some of the power drives a fan that pushes out air with the exhaust, thereby increasing thrust; used in most airliners as they are more economical and less noisy than turbojet engines

TURBOJET Simple type of gas turbine (jet) engine in which a compressor forces air into a combustion chamber where fuel is burned, and the hot gases produced spin a turbine which drives the compressor; noisier than turbofan engines used by most airliners

TURBOPROP Type of gas turbine engine connected to a propeller and used to power it (*see also* PROPELLER)

UNDERCARRIAGE An airplane's landing gear

VECTORED THRUST Way of moving an aircraft by swiveling its propellers or the tail-pipe of its jet engine so the thrust pushes the aircraft in another direction. Some airships and fighter-planes use vectored thrust.

WIDE-BODIED Name given to commercial airplanes with wide internal cabins, allowing for three sets of seating in each row and two aisles

WING-WARPING Control of an airplane's ability to bank or roll by torsion (twisting) of the outer wing edges instead of using ailerons.

YAW Turning movement to one side or the other made by adjusting an aircraft's rudder

Wide-bodied aircraft

Index

Acknowledgments

The publisher would like to thank:
Aeromega Helicopters, Stapleford, England: pp. 50-51, 52-53
Airship Industries, London: pp. 56-57; and especially Paul Davie and Sam Ellery
Bristol Old Vic Theatre, Bristol, England, for studio space: pp. 54-55, 60-61, 62-63; and especially Stephen Rebbeck
British Aerospace, Hatfield: pp. 34-35, 44-45
Cameron Balloons, Bristol, England: pp. 54-55; and especially Alan Noble
Musée des Ballons, Forbes' Chateau de Balleroy, Calvados, France: pp. 8-9
Noble Hardman Aviation, Crickhowell, Wales: pp. 26-27
Penny and Giles, Christchurch, England: p. 47 (flight data recorder)
RAF Museum, Hendon, London: pp. 16-17, 23, 24, 29, 38-39, 48-49, 52-53; and especially Mike Tagg
SkySport Engineering, Sandy, Bedford, England: pp. 18-19, 20-21; and especially Tim

Moore and all the team at SkySport
Rolls-Royce, Derby, England, pp. 36-37
Solar Wings Limited, Marlborough, England: pp. 60-61, 62-63; and especially John Fack
The Hayward Gallery, London, and Tetra Associates: pp. 6-7
The London Gliding Club, Dunstable, England: pp. 59-59; and especial thanks to Jack Butler
The Science Museum, London: pp. 10-11, 12-13, 25, 28-29, 30-31, 39, 40, 46-47; and especially Peter Fitzgerald
The Science Museum, Wroughton, England: pp. 32-33; and especially Arthur Horsman and Ross Sharp
The Shuttleworth Collection, Old Warden Aerodrome, Bedford, England: pp. 14-15, 22, 38, 40-41, 42-43; and especially Peter Symes

John Bagley of the Science Museum for his help with the text
Lester Cheeseman for his desktop publishing expertise

The publisher would also like to thank Ian Graham for his assistance on the paperback edition.

The publisher would also like to thank the following for their kind permission to reproduce their photographs:

Picture credits:
a=above, c=center, b=below, l=left, r=right, t=top
Airship Industries: 57br.
Austin J. Brown: 27tr; 35tr; 36tr; 55cl.
Aviation Images: Mark Wagner 65br, 68cr, 68bl.
BAA Picture Library/In-Press Photography: Anthony Charlton 69clb. **British Aerospace:** 35br, cr. **Corbis:** Galen Rowell 70tr; Karl Weatherly 70tl; Washington University 64br, Harmon: 53br. **Hulton Picture Library:** 9tc, br; 48tl; 52tr. **Jerry Young:** 55bl. **Mary Evans Picture Library:** 6tc, bl; 8bl; lltr, br; 141c; 15 rc; 20tl; 21br; 26tl; 32tl; 33br; 39br; 48l; 52tl; 53tl; 56tl; 64tr; G B Edwards 66cl. **Getty Images:**

Chris Salvo 69cla; Mark Wagner 68-69. **Michael Holford:** 10tc. **Hulton Archive/Getty Images:** 67cra. **Popperfoto:** 39tr; 53tr; 64bl, 67tl, 67clb; Reuters 67br. **Quadrant:** 49bc. **Retrograph Archive:** 61c. **Rex Features:** 65cla, 70-71; Dennis Stone 71br; Mega 70bl. **Robert Hunt Library:** 18bl. **Fred Sgrosso:** 68tr. **Solar Wings:** 60bl, 62bl. **The Science Museum, London:** 10bl; 12bc; 13br. **Topham Picturepoint:** 64tl, 66cra, 66bl; **Jonathan Wolfe/Skydyes:** 68tl; **Zefa:** 37br; 60tr, br.

Illustration by: Mick Loates, Peter Bull
Picture research by: Suzanne Williams

Jacket images:
Front: CB: © Jim Sugar/Corbis
Cl: © Reuters/Corbis

All other images © Dorling Kindersley.
For further information see:
www.dkimages.com